They Sent a Wumman

Nancy Nicolson

Nancy Nicolson – singer, songwriter, melodeon player, speaker, teacher, trainer or, if you wish, 'Cultural Crofter' – was brought up on a croft in Caithness. From behind the curtain in the box bed when she should have been sleeping, she used to hear her "Granda and his cronies yarning about poaching and illicit stills." She remembers there was water from the well, peats for fuel, and a pair of Clydesdales as the only horse-power on the croft, but that did not stop her being an Elvis fan and a rock-n-roller when she went to the dances in Wick.

Nancy studied at Edinburgh University and at Moray House Teacher Training College, and became a primary school teacher. She was a scriptwriter for BBC Scotland Schools Radio, worked with the New Makars Trust, writing songs with bairns in Fife, and was Education Officer with Celtic Connections.

Nancy came late to singing, believing, like so many others, that she could not sing. Aged 33, she began to sing at Edinburgh Folk Club, and soon after started to write songs and to play melodeon. While resident musician at the Royal Oak Folk Bar in Edinburgh, she was described by one regular as 'an instant ceilidh'. As writer, singer, storyteller, and animateur, Nancy Nicolson communicates the life and culture of Scotland with rare warmth and energy, and her own brand of wit and wisdom.

Cover Illustrations:

Cover Portrait
'The cover portrait is by my friend, the Polish artist Ewa Klejnowska-Allan, now living in Wick. She has a rare talent for catching the spirit of her subject. It is based on a photo by her husband Tom Allan, taken at a merry concert in the village of Keiss, North of Wick, in the Summer of 2016.' Nancy Nicolson

Back Cover
'"Flowers in the Sand" by Denness Morton, Nancy's husband of 46 years till he was stolen away in 2011. He still lives in this work, his anger at blood spilt on sand just spitting out of the paint.' Nancy Nicolson
Photo of Nancy and "Flowers in the Sand' by Allan McMillan.

They Sent a Wumman

The Collected Songs of
Nancy Nicolson

They Sent a Wumman:
The Collected Songs of Nancy Nicolson

Edited by Eberhard Bort
Typeset by Gonzalo Mazzei, Grace Note Publications

First published 2016 by Grace Note Publications C.I.C.
Grange of Locherlour, Ochtertyre, PH7 4JS, Scotland

books@gracenotereading.co.uk
www.gracenotepublications.co.uk

Songs, poems & story © Nancy Nicolson
Individual chapters © Contributors

ISBN 978-1-907676-86-4

This book is dedicated to
my darling daughters
Janet and Anna

ACKNOWLEDGEMENTS

This book is the first time Nancy Nicolson's songs are collected and published in book form. We acknowledge the great work by Brian Craib, providing the musical notation for the songs. Our thanks are also due to the Johnston Collection (see below) for allowing us to reproduce a selection from their astonishing photo archive. Of more modern vintage are the photos of Allan McMillan of Nancy Nicolson, singing at Edinburgh Folk Club, and the photo of Edinburgh's Festival Theatre. We are grateful to Ewa Klejnowska-Allan for her painting of Nancy, which graces the front cover, and to Nancy's late husband Denness Morton for his stunning painting 'Flowers in the Sand' on the back cover of this book, as well as for the line drawing 'The Road to the Croft' and the cartoon 'Mrs God'. We are chuffed to have permission to reproduce cartoons by Karrie Fransman and Steve Bell of the *Guardian* as very apt illustrations to Nancy's songs. Thanks also to Ewan McVicar for allowing us to reissue the songs of Nancy which appeared on *Rhyme and Reason* (Gallus, 1990). He, and George Gunn and Gerda Stevenson are to be congratulated on their splendid contributions to this volume.

The Johnston Collection

Eric Farquhar on the Photographs from a Unique Archive of Work by the Johnston Family in Wick

The Johnston photographer family captured an era when Wick was the herring capital of Europe. 'The Silver Darlings', as the herring were fondly known, attracted over a thousand boats which crowded into Wick harbour from June to September each year. Then thousands of migrant workers would swell the town population, and the Johnstons photographed them preparing their boats, setting sails, landing catches, gutting, curing, packing and carting the barrels of salt herring for export across the world. They fed the slaves of the West Indies as well as the peoples of Russia, Europe and as far down as

Ghana in West Africa. This is a unique pictorial record of Wick's growth and its importance as the major herring port, bigger than Amsterdam.

The collection also portrays the rural life of Caithness and North Sutherland, including the Kildonan gold rush. It shows castles and crofts, farming and flagstone and many of the characters and livestock that populated the surrounding countryside. The majority of the 50,000 surviving negatives are studio portraits of people from all over the UK. They are an invaluable tool for anyone with an interest in their family history.

Prints of the photos may be ordered from the website <www.johnstoncollection. net>.

Nancy is proud to present photos from the collection, and deeply grateful to the Wick Society for allowing their use in this book.

Alexander Johnston (1839-1896)
(© Johnston Collection)

CONTENTS

SONGS

I BAIRNS

POEMS AND A STORY

RHYME AND REASON

List of Illustrations

INTRODUCTION

Nancy Nicolson: The Cultural Crofter from Caithness

Eberhard Bort

It was the *Sunday Express* on 13 October 2013 that tried to open our eyes about the dangerous subversion perpetrated by a heap of Scottish songwriters. Education Scotland, it revealed,[1] was promoting 'a number of modern, politically-biased songs' for primary and secondary school pupils under the heading 'Freedom and Scots People'.[2] Among these singled out in the article were the late Hamish Henderson's 'The Freedom Come-All-Ye', Dick Gaughan's 'Both Sides the Tweed' (a co-write with James Hogg, but we'll let that pass), that 'modern' rebel rouser Robert Burns's 'Scots Wha Hae', John Mack, Morris Blythman and Jim McLean's 'Ding Dong Dollar', Billy Connolly's 'The Welly Boot Song', and – oor Nancy, with 'Who Pays the Piper?', her, as the paper had it, 'attack' on 'the "immensely rich companies" involved in the North Sea Oil industry.' A unionist politician was cited, calling the whole project 'an outrageous example of taxpayer funded political propaganda.' So be warned, the *Daily Express* might not approve of this publication either. Nancy Nicolson's reaction was typical – 'Oh to be in such company, that would be some pairty!'

I first met Nancy when I came to Edinburgh in 1995 to work at Edinburgh University. Where? In the Royal Oak, of course. Or was it at Edinburgh Folk Club? No matter, more than twenty years ago, Nancy was already part and parcel of the Edinburgh folk scene. And she was umbilically linked to both. At Edinburgh Folk Club she had the distinction of being the only songwriter to be barred from partaking in the annual songwriting contest – after having

---

[1] Ben Borland, 'Scottish pupils taught to sing for separation', *Sunday Express*, 13 October 2013.

[2] <www.educationscotland.gov.uk/scotlandssongs/secondary/index.asp>

won it three times in rapid succession. She has since repeatedly served as a judge in that competition. Nancy continues to be a regular floor singer at the Club, and has, from its inception in 2002, been involved in the Carrying Stream Festival, Edinburgh Folk Club's annual celebration of the life and legacy of Hamish Henderson, one of her mentors.

In the Oak, she had her own session, has been singing at the Wee Folk Club and Festival Folk at the Oak, and presented her own shows, working with the likes of Bobby Eaglesham, Billy Craib, Tony Mitchell, Alastair McDonald and Murray Macleod. *Three Weeks*, in a four-star review, wrote this about her 'Air Alba' Festival show:

> Nancy Nicolson ... enchants her audience in the Royal Oak's intimate venue with tales of childhood, Scottish folklore and, of course, Robert Burns. As she invites volunteers to share a dram you think of family and fireside story-sharing; this is an experience unlike any other, and one is left feeling oddly changed as the show ends and the spell breaks. Nancy's talk is informative, her songs [are] delightful. [...] you'll never feel more at home at the Fringe.[3]

One of the shows, 'Nancy's Whisky', recently acquired a new lease of life when Nancy was invited by the Pulteneytown People's Project to Wick to perform her songs, yarns and music of whisky, next door to, and sponsored by, Old Pulteney.

While a resident musician at the Royal Oak, Nancy was described by one regular as 'an instant ceilidh'. This, she assures me, still holds true. Impromptu ceilidhs have emerged around her at EIS conferences (frequently along with Robin Harper MSP), on commuter trains with Irish Rugby Fans and the connivance of the ticket collector, at numerous stage doors (inside with the staff, not outside busking) and at the drop of a hat in the Royal Oak, day or night.

In her own account and in George Gunn's contribution, it is evident how big a role both Edinburgh Folk Club and the Royal Oak played in creating the Nancy Nicolson whose songs are collected and published for the first time in

---

[3] < www.completemusicupdate.com/htmldaily/090819.html>

this volume. What also becomes abundantly clear is the love of a committed teacher to her bairns, the work for the New Makars Trust in Fife, and for Celtic Connection in Glasgow – pioneering work she cherished.

Like few others, Nancy Nicolson has the gift – as writer, singer and storyteller – to communicate the life and culture of Scotland, with rare warmth and energy and her very own brand of wit and wisdom. As can be seen in this volume, she covers (nearly) every subject under the sun – from bootleg whisky to the Miners' Strike, from bairns' play to the grim and cruel games of war, and from 'hauf-hangit' Maggie to 'Maggie's Pit Ponies'.

Nancy's lyrics, Karen Forbes observed, 'have a distinctive quality of fairness: giving a voice to those who might not otherwise be heard.'

> Many of Nancy's songs speak out for the 'underdogs' in society; those who cannot be heard above the din of the ruling classes or wealthy management. By imagining the feelings of the workers rather than just accepting the historical narrative, usually written by and for the cultural elite, Nancy politicises and vocalises the story of those who were written out of history...[4]

In her own words – her sleeve notes for the McCalman's version of 'Who Pays the Piper?' – her angry lament expressed loss and grief for the 167 oil men who died in the Piper alpha oil rig disaster in 1988:

> The money-wells in the North Sea are owned by immensely rich companies and fed by workers' lives. The men off-shore have to watch their tongues or lose their jobs. We can be their voices.[5]

And she is a sair fechter for the Scots language – particularly as spoken in her home county of Caithness. As Tom Knox remarked, 'it is ... reassuring to know that we have people of the talent and tenacity of Nancy Nicolson fighting to keep the Scots language on the cultural and political agenda.'[6]

---

[4] Karen Forbes, *Nancy Nicolson, Cultural Crofter*, Dissertation, submitted to the School of Scottish Studies, University of Edinburgh, May 2014, p.42.

[5] The McCalmans, *Flames on the Water*, Greentrax CDTRAX036, 1990.

[6] Tom Knox, *Nancy Nicolson: The Singer and the Songs*, Field Project/Scottish Ethnology II, School of Scottish Studies, University of Edinburgh, 2001.

Some of her songs have nearly become 'traditional' by now, being taken up by other singers – among them Nancy's greatest hits: ''Listen tae the Teacher', 'The Moon in the Morning', 'The Brickie's Ballad' and 'They Sent a Wumman'. Among others, Gerda Stevenson, The McCalmans and Ed Miller have recorded her songs. For this publication, an enhanced version of her 1990 tape, recorded and issued by Ewan McVicar, is included, with a handful of songs recently recorded by David O'Leary at Edinburgh Folk Club.

Nancy Nicolson, Cultural Crofter was the title of the dissertation by Karen Forbes. That is a very apt description for Nancy who is more than a folk singer or a tradition bearer, more than a songwriter or a storyteller or a melodeon player, as you are about to see when you enter these pages: the autobiographical piece by Nancy herself, George Gunn's contribution, based on a conversation with Nancy, Gerda Stevenson's reminiscences of collaborating with Nancy on her radio show, and Ewan McVicar's recollection of recording Nancy's songs form the backdrop – but the focus is firmly on the songs, in all their glorious diversity.

It was an immense pleasure to help putting this volume together. It involved a few sessions in Nancy's hospitable kitchen; and working again with the inspirational Gonzalo Mazzei of Grace Note Publications. A heartfelt thanks to all who contributed to the volume. It was, I hope you will agree, high time that Nancy Nicolson's songs were collected and published. That it now happens to mark her seventy-fifth birthday is as good a reason for a party as you'll get this year.

As Karen Forbes noted in her Dissertation, Nancy's introduction to the children at her workshops is 'I'll sing you a story and tell you a song'.[7] That'll do nicely as a motto for this book. Even at the risk of the *Sunday Express* taking offence, again.

---

[7] Forbes, p.2.

A CANNA SING!

Nancy Nicolson

This Book is for You

My name is Nancy. **I can sing**
1. I sing.
2. I make songs.
3. I perform in clubs and on stages.

If, when I was thirty, you had suggested even one of these to me, never mind three, I'd have argued, quibbled, told you that you were daft, and more than likely laughed in your face.

But I dare to say it now. It was neither advancing age nor my own self-belief that made the difference, that made me a singer; it was the friends and colleagues who could see in me what I refused to see myself. And, Oh, am I grateful to them for the love of singing that they inspired in me!

But why should this be of interest to anybody but myself?

You may well ask. To write about oneself looks like an exercise in self-glorification, in vanity. I confess there may be a bit of that, something for which I ought to apologise. However, there is another reason that I believe justifies the pen in my hand.

It is the belief that if I can do such things, then anybody can.

You can.

Maybe you do sing, write and perform. Brilliant. You make the world a richer, warmer place.

In that case, I hope you will find here a song to sing, or a lyric to read that will interest you.

But what if you don't sing? What if you are wont to say, 'Don't ask me to sing. I'll clear the room'?

If that is the case, then this book is truly for you.

Language

Now a tangent, a change of subject, or as ma Mam used til say, 'Off o eygs on til tatties'.

Do you speak Caithness? If not, no worries, on p 61-63 there is a Caithness Language Primer, but here's your starter for ten, or nearer twenty, words and phrases I use throughout:

> **A or Ah-** I; **aat or at,** that; **A canna**–I can't; **an**–and; **chiel**–man; **eygs**–eggs; **fey**-from; **heidie**– headmaster; **Kaitness**–Caithness; **ken**–know; **lok**–lot; **mind/mind on** – remember; **ma**-my; **o**–of; **peedie**-little; **tatties**–potatoes; **til**–to; **wi**-with

When you sing you listen, you employ words, you use a language and an accent.

Anyone who travels through Scotland cannot but notice the rich and magnificent variety of spoken language. The shapes of the inflections are like a melody with the vowel sounds as notes, shifting with every ten miles you travel. Here I am writing in standard English. That is what we are taught in school, what is used in print media, newspapers and magazines, and spoken on radio and TV. It is a grand, handsome and historic language.

Code Drift

For the last fifty years I have lived in Edinburgh, frequently travelling North, Far North, to Caithness, the flat land East beyond the Highlands. It was described by a nineteenth-century traveller as 'Caithness, that fine county, separated from the Highlands by the great moorland of The Ord and joined to Orkney by the sea.' I have never heard a more apt definition.

I go from Edinburgh to Newton, the scattered crofting township where I grew up, and to Wick where I went to school. For many years I had been only vaguely aware that I changed my speech as I travelled. I was conscious of it when, as a student, I was taking Denness, my Edinburgh – or rather Leith – boyfriend home to meet the family. Denness told me later that as we got on the train at Waverley Station I was speaking as I normally did, in everyday English with the North accent that he loved. By the time we got to Inverness he wondered what was happening. The words and the way I spoke were changing. Even the sounds I made seemed to come from a darker, deeper part of my head. By the time we got off the train at Wick he could hardly understand a word I said.

This phenomenon had come up in fourth-year in Wick High School with English Teacher John Ross. He was regaling us with the glories of Caithness Language. Then he spoke of the facility that some people have in 'leaning towards' a dialect or accent that they spend time with. I had noticed it in myself when staying with cousins in Latheron, all of sixteen miles south of Newton. There the accent is heavily influenced by a people who used to speak Gaelic. Instead of saying 'I am going *up* to *Lath*eron on the *bus*,' they said, 'I am going *i-ip* to *La-ath*eron in the *bi-is*'. It was said in a soft, gentle way, with the long vowels of the Gael. By the time I had stayed for three weeks I returned to Newton speaking 'Latheron'. Later I found this happened at University where my best pal was from Orkney. Just an hour with Dot Harcus had my phrases lifting at the end and vowels drifting North. John Ross said it was a characteristic of effective listeners who were receptive to the language around them. Later, at Moray House Teacher Training College, I found it had an official designation: 'Code Drift'.

Growin up atween languages lek A did, there is a lok o 'Code Drift' goin on.

Fey now onwards, esteemed reader, I will drift code, meander fey Caithness Scots til Scots-English til Standard English. And no, I canna define them for ye. Ye are smert enough til work aat oot for yersel. An many's the time I will speak o Kaitness, ma favoured way til spell e neyme o ma ain County. It's no consistent, but if ye want consistency, ye'd better be goin til a baking class wi e WRI – wur treasured Women's Rural Institute.

First influences in words and language were Mam and Dad of coorse, but no far behind were Granny Stewart and Granda Nicolson. Granny was wont to sing the big classic Scots Ballads, not in company, but when we were in the hoose wursels. She sang 'Sir Patrick Spens'. I was greatly taken by the image of 'the new moon wi the old moon in her airms'. We often witnessed that phenomenon in wur great big black dark Kaitness skies. That wis Granny Stewart, Mam's Mam. Granda Nicolson was Dad's Dad. He didna sing, but he was a great one for givin bairns a 'sail' on his back, a 'sail' on his bike or a 'sail' on the horse. I was into my twenties before I realised that 'sail' was our Maritime County's equivalent to the word 'ride' for being on a bike, a horse or a Granda! Cousins in Edinburgh were bamboozled by the usage.

Dungarees

I am happy that I remember some elements of my childhood very clearly. I can pinpoint what happened before and after I was four when we flitted, in a henhouse, from Toftcarl Fairm Cottage to the Newton croft to live with Granda Nicolson. I can mind clearly which events took place where.

Long before I was four I loved listening to folk speaking and would ponder over words. Two in particular fascinated me. They were 'waterproof' and 'dungarees'. (Aye, interested in clothes even then). I jaloused how these words came to be. For 'waterproof' I heard 'water-poor-off', so it was a coat for the water to pour off! 'Dungarees' was even more fun. We said 'Downg-greez'. Ma Dad wore them workin in e byre on e fairm, an his freend Jimmy wore them in e shed sortin e tractor. Dad wis muckin oot downg an Jimmy wis working wi greez, downg an greez – dung and grease, hence 'downg-greez' or 'dungarees'. Simple. Rational. Brilliant. There I was, a bairn, creating an etymology for interesting words. I'm speaking here about me, but I'm no exception, no phenomenon. All bairns do this in their own space and place, in their own family and society.

The root of that skill is listening. Bairns are fabulous listeners, as you will know if you've ever said something out of turn that a bairn heard and repeated in an embarrassing moment.

Mam

I can mind listening, listening to ma Mam singing.

Again, a wee tangent, this time to focus on the sophistication of the thought processes of peedie bairns. Folk too readily assume they don't have a developed understanding. Folk are sorely mistaken. The bairns understand far more than may be imagined.

In Toftcarl ma Mam used to sing, but only when there was nobody else around. She claimed later, when asked to sing at New Year, that she could not sing. I knew better. She used to sing a popular song from the wireless, sung I think by Delia Murphy.

> *Let him go, let him tarry, let him sink or let him swim,*
> *He doesn't care for me and I don't care for him.*
> *He can go and get another that I hope he will enjoy,*
> *For I'm going to marry a far nicer boy.*
>
> *He can go to his old mother and set her heart at ease,*
> *She's a grim and girnin wumman, and very hard to please*
> *It's slighting me and talking ill is what she's always done*
> *All for that I was coortin her great big ugly son.*

I enjoyed the tune and learned it instinctively, but more than that, I appreciated the words, the story. There was me, all of four years old, loving the attitude of this girl. I did not know the word 'attitude', but that's what I admired. I had a young auntie with friends who met at wur hoose before going to dances. I was perfectly aware of situations anent girl-friends and boy-friends.

As I have said, bairns are experts in language. They learn the essential words and structure of a whole language without any formal lessons. They hear, they listen, they repeat, they make sense of it.

So ma Mam could sing. But something convinced her she couldna an she shouldna sing. She needed support, and I ken who could have provided it. Just one wee problem there. He had lived at the other end of the country and 150 years before.

Burns and Betsy

Throughout my life I have taken up a variety of causes, have campaigned for deserving issues, and have revelled in some fine comrades-in arms.

I claim kinship and common cause with Robert Burns in my wish to have the songs of the people saved – saved not only in books, but to be sung live, in company, in revelry and on stages.

Burns first. I was living just over the top of Newton Hill, a mile from the market and fishing town of Wick in Caithness in the far North-east of Scotland. In these days many families read a weekly magazine called *Picture Post*. We did not buy it ourselves, just got it the following week when our neighbour Jim Kennedy brought it down on his Monday night visit. Magazines were a luxury too far for us, with Granda, Mam, Dad and three bairns living on Dad's £5 weekly wage of a farm servant.

My favourite feature was the full-page colour picture. This might be a photo of a member of the Royal Family or a Film Star. Sometimes it was of a famous painting. I loved looking for the picture. Once, or maybe more than once, it was a painting of a bonnie man with sideburns, soft dark brown hair and the most beautiful deep, shining eyes. My great Aunt Betsy had cut out the picture and pasted it on the wall of her peedie thatched hoosie nearby. She saw the six-year-old Nancy gazing at it, rapt, and told me this man was Robert Burns, a fine fairmer who wrote songs. There was one called 'Ca the Yowes tae the Knowes'. Her daughter Bunty sang it for me. I loved it. I kent what yowes were, and soon worked out that knowes were hilly bitties o ground. I recognised the song when folk sang it in the hoose at New Year. But Mam never joined in. How I wish that Mam had met Jean Redpath.

In the eighties, although I did sing bey then, I still felt insecure about it. In the school notices I saw an advert for a Summer School at Stirling University with Jean Redpath to study Burns Song, Ballads and Bairns' song. It looked just what I needed. The course literature claimed we would study the songs. We did study them, but mainly Jean's aim was to have us **sing** them. Classes were punctuated by her resounding command – **'SING!'** Anyone who has studied with her will recognise the order, and hear it explode on the air. She worked ceaselessly to have folk secure in their own right and ability to sing. She would ask folk why they believed they could not sing. A number replied it was because teachers, friends or family said they sounded awful or were out of tune. Jean's response was, 'They said that? That's THEIR problem. Never mind them!' Yes, I claim community with wonderful accomplices. Jean Redpath and Robert Burns, and their beliefs have accompanied me on many an outing, as indeed they do on the campaign I pursue here and now.

School

Mind the peedie lassie who worked out the etymology of dungarees?

Came the day when she, as all bairns must, entered the education system. The Education System is where all the original thinking, imagination and mental magic are knocked out of bairns. In their place will be hammered in coarse, lumpen, inadequate instructions, rote learning, rules and lessons with, top o the list, the requirement for obedience and assimilation. She, of course, was me. And maybe you. All bairns have a brilliant creative mind BEFORE they go to school.

Fan A furst geed off til e school A geed ower e peedie hillie, doon e beeg Newton brey, ower e breeg on e burn an in til e toon. But fan A got in til e toon an inside e school, A fun at wis no fit A'd done at aal on ma rod til e Academy School.

They spoke another language. I learned the other language.

I 'ought' to have said, 'When I first went off to school I went over the little hill, down the big Newton hill, over the bridge on the stream and into town'.

The way the teachers spoke was strange, weird, entirely different from the language around us at home. Before we went to school we had been warned within an inch o *wur* lives til do fit e teycher said. Id wiz, 'Don't ye come hom here an tell me yu're in trouble wi e teycher or ye'll get a looger'. Listen til e teycher. Do fit ye're tellt.'

And that was it. If the teacher spoke that funny posh way, aal perchink, then we 'knew' we just had to do the same thing, no argument. No point sayin anything til Mam and Dad.

Soon I had taken on the mantle of 'Do as you are told' to the point where teachers considered me 'a good girl, a clever girl'. I grant I was obedient. But clever? I was among the oldest in the class, so was just that bit more mature and able to comprehend school ways. I listened to the teacher and parroted back to her what she told the class. Hardly clever, but it meant that teachers approved and expected a lot of me. I was first in the class. Folk would say 'Ye're a clever lassagie. Are ye goin til be a teycher?' I answered in horror with a determined 'NO-OH!' I didna ken fit I wanted til be, but I was sure I **never** wanted til be a teycher!

One day, aged 7, in Miss Tait's class, we were studying sentences. 'Give me a sentence', she said, 'a long sentence about something you did yesterday.' I pondered a bittie then put my hand up. 'Yesterday when I got home from the school I fed the hens, and one of the hens flew up onto the hen-hoose roof.' The second I said 'hoose' I was horrified with myself. Miss Tait nailed me with an icy glare... silence from the whole class... then 'HOOSE!' she thundered. I shrank, mortified. Maybe she did not notice, but I did not volunteer an answer again for weeks.

Her 'correcting' my language did not make me speak better English. It stopped me speaking at all!

I retold the story in the song 'Listen tae the Teacher'. To my delight it is now included in Education Scotland's 'The Kist', a repository of writing for the curriculum in Scottish Schools. That is a sweet revenge! Thinking of it now, I have a sneaking sympathy for Miss Tait. She had been trained and drilled to knock 'slang' out of her pupils. I wish I had a chance to tell her it's not 'slang'... 'it's language'.

Teachers made oot they knew everything. We kent they didna. They never said a word aboot fairming, croftin or fishin. They were like half-people that only kent aboot half o the world they lived in. They could never have guessed that a sizeable group of their seemingly biddable and obedient bairns held them in deepest disdain!

Everything was prim and prissy, especially in 'Singing'. When we were seven we were taken to a fine room with a piano for 'Singing' with Singing Teacher Mrs Clark. She was large, well-corseted and bosomy, with a tweed skirt, shiny silk stockings and high-heeled brown lace-up shoes. She told us she wanted us all to sing 'prettily', that is, high, sweet and, as I considered it, squeaky. We sang 'Where the bee sucks, there lurk I'. And 'Now is the Month of Maying when Merry Lads are Playing'. Then one day we got a new song book. Mrs Clark said, "Turn to page 23, a song by Robert Burns, 'Ca the Yowes tae the Knowes'." You could have knocked me down with a feather! That Mrs Clark, of all teachers, knew about Caain Yowes tae the Knowes! I was totally won over, and we fair gave it laldy on all the Scots songs; 'Loch Lomond', 'Ye Banks and Braes', 'The Wee Cooper o Fife', 'The Mingulay Boat Song'. Suddenly, Singing was the favourite lesson. I enjoyed the songs, their melodies and wonderful stories. Then came time for the annual Caithness

Music Festival of Music and Drama. Every school in Caithness selected pupils to sing solo and in choirs for this competitive event. I hoped quietly that I might be picked to sing solo, but was not chosen. I hoped that I might be picked for the choir, but was not chosen. I was deeply disappointed; even, to be honest, deeply hurt. I'd believed I could sing. But I was an oldest child, realistic, plain, sensible, ordinary. I had not been chosen. Clearly I was not a sufficiently good singer. No argument. FACT.

I took that fact on bravely, faced up to it and got on with my life. I could still sing when I was by myself, walking up Newton Brae, or goin oot til get e coos in for milkin.

Santa and God

I was disillusioned with teachers. In some areas of life that disillusion extended to all adults. Take, for instance, the case of Santa Claus and God. You may consider that these are two odd personages to link together, but just you hing on, there's a tale to tell.

I first remember Christmas and Santa when I was three in the cottage at Toftcarl. I mind wakening up in my wee trundle bed in the kitchen, looking over to the fireplace and seeing a present! It was a Rocking horse. The following year it was a two-storey Doll's house, perfect even to the match-stick slats on the shutters. Now Mam and Dad had next to no money. Where had the Christmas presents come from, fine, hand-crafted wooden toys? They had been made by the prisoners of war in Watten, in the centre of Caithness.

I thought Santa must be a fine mannie. Every Christmas the local Women's Rural Institute ran a party, 'The Christmas Treat', in each rural school. Santa was always there, in big boots, red coat with white fur, and his great big white beard. We kent aboot Santa. The folk we loved told us that if were good Santa would bring us a present, and if we were bad, then he wouldna. Santa, I reckoned, was not very good at knowin fit folk were doing. I kent plenty bairns doing mischievious, even plain bad things. But they all got a present. Years passed. Now I was a big girl of eight at the Tannach Christmas Treat. It was fine to meet all the other bairns. John and Margaret, David Innes, and a whole lok o Stevens. Came the moment for lights out, then the jingle of bells, and Ho-Ho-Ho, the door burst open. There was Santa Claus! He even came an sat beside me. I didna want to be cheeky, to stare at his face, so my eyes wandered to his boots. They were big rubber boots, North British the company name on them, wi a pattern o sharn around the feet. Weel weel, Santa must be a fairmer, or a crofter, I jaloused. And look, just above the sharn there was a right-angled nick in the rubber.. Santa must hev been climmin a fence and cut it on the barbed weer. Santa was a real chiel wi a real job. I was impressed.

We all got wur presents, Santa bade fareweel, and we danced 'The Grand Old Duke of York'. After a whilie, David Innes's Dad came in. He laughed and played and then he sat beside me. My eyes fell on his boots. We-e-ll. His boots hed a pattern o sharn on them, and just abeen that ... a peedie right-angled nick, the kind ye'd get if ye'd cut id in a barbed weer fence! Came the slow, sad, realisation and resignation. There wis no Santa. Iss Santa wis just David Innes' Dad dressed up in fancy dress. Was I surprised? No that much. I wasna even that disappointed. The world, I was finding, was a disappointing place. Get used til id, Nancy.

Now at eight I was big enough to go to the Sunday school. It was better than real school, but not much more fun. God and Jesus turned out to be a bittie like Mam when she was sending me to the school. In all the stories God and Jesus seemed to say, 'Do as ye are tellt. Don't do bad things'. Well, that made sense. Ye shouldna do bad things. Then they said that if ye were good, ye'd get til go til Heaven when ye dee'd. I was no too keen thinkin aboot deein – and why did God think he hed til bribe us til be good? We'd be good anyway.

A year or two passed. Now, at 10 or 11, I was a 'big one', a trusted one. In the Sunday School, I looked efter the peedie wans, carried the collection to Mr Sinclair, and sometimes did the readings in the kirk service. But all the time I was thinkin aboot God ... and aboot Santa. I couldna help seein parallels. I'm not sure whether I was the more fascinated or sad as they began to add up:

Santa: a beeg mannie wi a white beard, at lives in a far-off place fill o white snow.

God: a beeg mannie wi a white beard, at lives in a far-off place fill o white clouds.

Santa's helpers: lassagies who could fly. They were dressed in white, wi gossamer wings.

God's helpers: lassagies who could fly. They were dressed in white, wi feather wings.

Santa wanted: aal e bairns til be good. If they were good, they got presents. If no, they got none.

God wanted: aal e fowk til be good. If they were good, they went til Heaven when they dee'd. If no, they went til Hell.

Id hed til be more than coincidence. I looked at different paintings of God. Every wan hed a different face. A real God couldna hev dizzens o different faces.

I thought of the Santas I had seen. They were all different. Tall, short, thin, fat, all wi different voices.

Id wis e same deal. There wis no Santa. There wis no God.

They were just 'made up'.

Other Places, Other Bairns

So I was disillusioned wi the grown-up fowk. However, I did have instances, albeit half a lifetime later, when workin as an Early Years teacher wi young bairns, that restored, nay rebuilt, my faith in human nature.

The New Makars' Trust was a project led by Fifer Gifford Lind to write songs with schools. In 1980 I was working at Headwell, a special primary school in Dunfermline, for children with a variety of disabilities. There to my delight I found evidence of the generous, complex and world-aware nature of the thinking of young children.

It was coming up to Christmas. I planned we make a song to the tune of the Gaelic Carol 'The Christ-child's Lullaby'. I asked the bairns if they had all the money and all the power in the world what they would wish for Christmas. The resulting song knocked me back in astonishment at their awareness of the needs of others around the world. They themselves might have wished for new legs or hands, or abilities – or for the toys being so seductively advertised on TV. Did they? Take a look at the song 'A Wish for the World'. They addressed the third-world issues of clean water, of homes and education for all.

In 2008, I encountered an astonishing example of not only factual memory, but of a child's appreciation of a situation that manifested itself a full 20 years after the original incident. Karrie was in my first class in Edinburgh in 1988, a primary 2 with lots of fascinating characters. Karrie, it turns out, had a prodigious memory. I discovered this twenty years later, on 5 Sept 2008, when I came face to face with myself in a strip cartoon on the back of the *Guardian* newspaper. I had sat down to do the (easy) crossword. My eye was drawn to the cartoon strip underneath, of wee ones in a school assembly, looking up to a Headmaster and a Teacher on the stage. It looked familiar. I was stunned to realise that the school was my own Edinburgh school, and the teacher was me. After twenty years Karrie Fransman had caught an astonishing resemblance of both me and Heidie. He, a great one for Scots tradition, had had me sing a song at Assembly. He was a good man, a committed Labour voter and no friend of Mrs Thatcher. The song was 'Don't Call Maggie a Cat'. In it I chide people who called Mrs T by animals' names. Among the animals, I cite a she-dog, a bitch. I believe that the Heidie wanted to demonstrate that 'bitch' was not necessarily a swear word. I suspect his real reason was to have a wee 'go' at Mrs T! I have since caught up with Karrie, and we've had some barrie blethers.

Edinburgh

Edinburgh ... Edinburgh ... Edinburgh.

Me an Mam are goin til Edinburgh – on e train!

I was six. I'd never been to Edinburgh. But far more important than that, I was goin on e train. I'd never been on a train. We'd go through our flat Caithness land, down to Inverness and then through the Highlands.

The high point would be crossing the Forth Bridge. Mam had shown me pictures of it. Oh, that was going to be such fun! At Wick Railway Station we got on the train, along the corridor and into the plush-seated compartment of three seats facing three seats. There were windows you could open. It was considered good luck to throw a silver coin from the window into the Forth. On approach to the Breeg I got my sixpence ready. Mam hed a shilling. As soon as we were above the water, Mam flung hers in and I flung mine, each making a wish. Mam had tellt me the wish must be a secret. Mine was so secret I canna mind what it was. The thrill of being on a train and on the bridge was dampened by one fact, the fact that has disappointed bairns for as long as trains have crossed. Take a look at the picture of that Bridge. Three wonderful arches, up and down, up and down, up and down.

The first time I took a Primary 3 class on a trip to Fife and we reached the other side of the Bridge I saw two bleak wee faces. 'What's wrong, James, what's wrong, Sarah? 'What is it?'

James answered, '... The train just went straight through ... I thought it went up an doon over the top!' I comforted them.

I kent how they felt.

My next trip to Edinburgh was different – aged eighteen, off to University. We'd left from Wick, five classmates from The High School: Alasdair, Shirley, Robert, Ruairidh and myself. There was the change and a long wait at Inverness. Isn't there always? We were about to go into the station cafe when Robert said. 'We're no goin there', and led us into the Station Hotel. We entered the stunning foyer and stood amazed. Robert took us to a window table and ordered coffee and cakes. We sat there in glory, enjoying the beautiful staircase, the one that was reputedly the model for the staircase of the Titanic. From then on this was a treasured feature of our journeys. That station cafe has never seen one of us yet. I still travel by train, up to four double trips a year, and always stop off at the Station, now the Royal Hotel, and remember our touch of style, and Robert, now sadly gone.

After the Station Hotel coffee, we parted company, the other three to Aberdeen, Alasdair and I to Edinburgh, Eventually, we reached The Capital, and a whole new world.

My course at University was for a degree in Pure Maths and Physics. Pure purgatory, more like. I had been strong-armed into this course as a result of a massive push by the Caithness Education Authority and the United Kingdom Atomic Energy Authority to supply nuclear physicists for the brand new Dounreay Experimental Reactor on the North Coast of Caithness. I was an obedient, passive creytur in school, and went along with the advice, assuming it was in my best interests. In due time exam results came: disaster! Against all my former intentions that I would **never** be a teacher, I switched to Moray House College to train as a Primary Teacher. I didn't mind what I did as long as I could pass the exams and save face for my Mam and Dad. For them I would even do this. I couldna hev fowk thinkin I'd been a Failure! The Teachers' college experience was to amaze me. It was three years of true learning. To my surprise I found that it was interesting and fulfilling to work with bairns, and I decided that Primary Early Years was my favourite stage.

The Crowd

The best thing by far about Moray House was meeting Dorothy Harcus from Orkney. I was behind this girl in the queue to register. Her clothes looked pretty daring for the ultra-conservative rules of the College: a wildly fuzzy purple mohair sweater over skin-tight green trousers, topped by a mop of bright red curly hair, rosy cheeks and a sparkling smile. Dot was part of large group of students from Orkney and Shetland. I was pleased to be welcomed as one of 'The Crowd'. They had all known each other from six years of Inter-island Sports, and this was now cemented by their six voyages a year to and from University on the MV *St Clair*. She sailed Lerwick – Kirkwall – Aberdeen – Leith. Dockings and departures were great fun.

Among this set of grand freens, with skilled guidance from Dot, I learned at the age of eighteen to be silly, to be happy, and even to do daft things. I was learning to be young instead of being the big sister, wifie-ish, over-responsible sometime spoilsport I had been at home. However, I was still the one they called on when a calm head was required. One such occasion was at a term-end, seeing the Islanders off on The *St Clair* at Leith.

We had gathered at Bill's Bar on the Shore. To use the old phrase, a number drank 'not wisely but too well'. One lad slipped from the bar stool to the floor. A big lad tried to pick him up, but he appeared boneless, slithering through the friend's hand like so much quicksilver. How were we to get him to the boat? The big chiel turned to me. 'Nancy, can ye do something?' I knew not what they thought I could do. Then I remembered there was a policeman on the Dock Gate. Dot and I went out to appeal to him. 'Na, Na, lasses, no another drunken islander. I'm no carryin one more o them on to a boat!' 'But what can we do?' I asked.

'We-e-ll,' he said, sucking air in through his teeth, 'There's your solution', and he pointed to the green door of a shed. I went over, opened the door to find a wheelbarrow, a green wheelbarrow! I took the handles, me dressed for a night out, in full make-up, frothy skirt, stiletto heels, and swinging ponytail.

I wheeled the barrow along the river and into the Bar. The Crowd loaded our boy into it, and he was duly conveyed to the ship and up the gangway. This particular gentleman went on to be a significant officer of the Transport Department of Shetland Islands Council. Fitting, I'd say!

Fit's Folk Music?

'The Crowd' provided my introduction to Folk Music, a genre I was not previously aware of. This was despite my having a Dad who played the pipes, an Uncle who was a top accordionist and a Granny who sang ballads. At the start of student third year Dot and I acquired a flat – well, flat may be gilding the lily somewhat: it was a third-floor room-and-kitchen opening straight off the lobby where we shared a loo with two families. But it was our own.

On the first night, surrounded by half-unpacked cases, Dot said, 'Nancy, The Crowd is going to the Crown.'

The conversation continued thus:

N: Fit's e Crown?
D: Its a bar. There's Folk Music.

N: Fit's Folk Music?
D: It's owld tunes and owld songs.

N: That disna sound much fun. Ye go. I'll just stay here. And so I did.
At about quarter past ten, Dot's curly head poked round the door.
D: Nancy?

N: Dot?
D: Nancy, wid it be aal right if we hed a perty some night?

N: Yes, of course.
D: That's fine, then, ... there's thirty folk comin up the stair.

Weel, it wasna quite thirty folk, but we had a braw party anyway. Every Tuesday night thereafter we were up til the small hours with the likes of Doli Maclennan, Archie and Ray Fisher, Owen Hand, Wattie Wright, Maggie and Liz Cruickshank, Josh Macrae and many more. You may well recognise a number of them. If you don't, they are worth a wee Google. On Thursdays the Crown hosted a Blues Club and we occasionally had the 'après-ski' of Robin Williamson, Bert Jansch and Clive Palmer who were to form the Incredible String Band. The Crown was a real cultural stew-pot. Where is it? It and all of Lothian Street were demolished to make the road that flies around Bristo Square and the Edinburgh Students' Union. Of the folk we met that night, Doli Maclennan and Liz and Maggie Cruickshank became firm friends. Doli introduced us to the Waverley Bar in St Mary's Street. Soon I was a barmaid in the upstairs, folk-singing bar. A lovely group played Friday Nights. I remember having to pay them – £3 between them. They were called the Corries. Bill, Roy and Ronnie were brilliant. Paddie Bell sang with them sometimes. We had visitors from abroad too. My favourite was the fabulous, mischievious, Alex Campbell.

I Meet Ma Man

Many of us from the North were as fond of a dance as we were of drinking. Leith figured largely in our lives. One night Dot and I went to a dance in Leith Town Hall, hoping to meet two lads we fancied. No luck. No lads. However, near the end of the night four good-looking guys in black suits and bow ties appeared. A Scottish Dance Band after a gig. One of them came over to me. 'May I have this dance?' he asked. I accepted and, as we moved together he said, 'I'm sorry, I'm not a very good dancer'. 'No a good dancer?', I thought, 'well, that's you finished before we start'. Still, he was bonnie, and grand to talk to. He asked to see me home. I said yes he could – as long as he saw my friend Dot home too. He took us both to Pilrig Street where I lived and then went to Warriston Crescent with Dot. And that is how I met my Leith Man, drummer and artist, Denness Morton, son of a Leith Docker. He did learn to dance for the 'Bride's Waltz' at our wedding the following year. Nancy Nicolson became Mrs Anne Hamilton Morton.

Edinburgh Folk Club

One day some years later, married and babied, I was at home in Edinburgh's Newington wi ma wee pets, Janet and Anna. The wireless, BBC Radio Scotland, mentioned a Folk Club in George Square. Denness was happy to look after the girls while I went to find 'The Edinburgh Folk Club'. It was in a basement. As I hovered at the top of the steps, I saw someone at the foot – Maggie Cruickshank, from Crown bar days. 'Nancy Nicolson!' she said. 'Where have you been hiding?' I was tickled to hear my name as Nancy Nicolson after seven years of being Mrs Morton.

Back home I mentioned it to Denness. He said, 'I always think of you as Nancy Nicolson. It was Nancy Nicolson I married. If somebody says Mrs Morton I think they mean my mother.' Thus we revived the old rural custom of calling a married wumman by her maiden name.

Edinburgh Folk Club proved a wonderful place for me, to find old friends and to enjoy the songs. I met John Barrow, the moving spirit of the Club, and Hamish Henderson, scholar, writer, soldier and pacifist. Maggie used to encourage me to get up and sing but, according to myself, I 'could not sing' and would not try.

My girls were getting bigger, now both at school, and in 1975 I resumed my work as a teacher with a primary 3 class in Midlothian. Now, with a class of seven-year–olds there are times when a song is needed. There, in my own classroom, wi my own bairns, I felt secure. Sufficiently secure to sing with them – 'Five little Speckled Frogs', 'Three Craws Sat upon a Wa', 'The Miners' Lullaby'. In a room with hard floors, walls and ceiling, the acoustic was good. The bairns loved singing, and I was tickled when wee Amanda said, 'Hey, Miss, you are a lovely singer.' When I thought about it I had to admit I sounded OK. That was the day I realised that *I could sing*. I was maybe even a decent singer. It was like winning the Lottery, something I had never dared hope for, an idea I had resisted for nearly thirty years.

I am still thinking of readers who insist that they cannot sing.

Are you sure? Or is it rather that you will not sing because you fear that someone will deem you to be 'not good enough'? Maybe the only 'someone' doing that is yourself. And if anyone else did, well, as Jean Redpath says, that's their problem, not yours!

In the following weeks at the Folk Club I plucked up courage, gave in to Maggie's wheedling and John Barrow's invitations to take a song, and became a 'floor singer'. The Folk Club was now a precious part of my life. Time rolled on. Attendance at the club had begun to wane. Hamish Henderson and John Barrow came up with a plot to engender new interest. The Club was to hold a Song-Writing Competition. I believe I mind John announcing: 'Ye've aal tae write a song'. I'd never written a song. But I had written cheeky Valentines to teachers at the High School (none of whom ever suspected the calm, sensible Nancy). Now the Edinburgh Folk Club had to survive. The club needed songs. I must write a song.

'Granda Said'

What could I write about? I cast around and remembered my Granda Nicolson teasing a six-year-old Nancy before my first visit to Edinburgh. He had told me to look for monsters with two tails at the Zoo, for two-legged rats in the streets, and for things called tram-cars. I would make Granda the subject of my song. Hence 'Granda Said'. The judges were Hamish Henderson, Alastair Clark, the *Scotsman* journalist, and Kenny Thomson, *Daily Record* Journalist and another organiser of the Club. I was amazed and delighted when they awarded me second prize. The winner was Sheila Douglas's gorgeous piece 'O, Mither, Mither'. I liked that song so much I recorded it on *Rhyme and Reason*, the cassette that Ewan McVicar produced for me in 1990. At the competition, people were lovely to me, praising 'Granda Said', the way I sang it, and my general presentation. I was amazed and delighted. I was embarrassed too. I had to insist I was not anything special. The on-stage apparent ease was an element of being a school teacher. Teachers are on a stage every day they go to work. You learn to make it work. You get used to it.

So I could sing. I could write a song. As I made more songs I was invited to appear on campaigning platforms. When or where I don't remember, but it was a signal day when I first met Ewan McVicar. He is another without whom I would never have been the writer and singer I am. He tells in his generous piece 'Getting Nancy's Songs Down on Tape' how he manoeuvred me into making the cassette *Rhyme and Reason*. To say I was pleased is to call Ben

Nevis a wee hillie! It was pure delight working with him, with Derek Moffat and the others. It's not modest of me, but I still take a listen to that CD and it lifts me every time. Ewan, you are a magician! *Rhyme and Reason* built me up and charged me to get on with writing more songs. My apologies to Ewan that I never went on to do 'that next CD'. Well, there were 33 sum books to correct!

Politics and Teachers' Union

Now, I never promised this story would be in chronological order. Good job too.

From 1976 I was teaching by day in Midlothian, and would do so for thirteen years. I would defy anyone to work in Midlothian and not become political.

There I got in tow with the active element of the Teachers' Union, The Educational Institute of Scotland, the EIS. We campaigned for the abolition of the belt, the dreaded Lochgelly strap that was still in use for corporal punishment; for an anti-nuclear stance in all areas; for parity in pay between primary and secondary teachers and many other needful issues. Union members were delighted to find a Primary One teacher willing to stand for the governing Board of the Union, the EIS General Council, There was under-representation of the primary sector in the higher echelons of the Union. However my Primary Heidie thought it was ridiculous that I was standing. Not only did I stand. I even came top of the poll. It's wicked of me to mention it, but I will: He himself stood.... and he came last in the poll!

In that era there was a strand of Primary Heidies who considered the EIS their own domain. I wrote a wee squib for such as he.

I'll butter ma breid on baith sides, Eat ma cake an huv it,
Ah'm the Heidie, Ah'm the boss, I run the EIS,
I'll butter ma breid on baith sides, Eat ma cake an huv it,
A'm the Heidie, A'm the boss, Jine the Heidie Tong.

Ye neednae wark, ye neednae strike, Buy a Rover, no a bike,
Transfer the staff ye dinnae like, Viva Heidie Tong!

> *I'll butter ma breid on baith sides, Eat ma cake an huv it,*
> *A'm the Heidie, A'm the boss, I run the EIS,*
> *I'll butter ma breid on baith sides, Eat ma cake an huv it,*
> *A'm the Heidie, A'm the boss, Jine the Heidie Tong*

Midlothian EIS were solidly left-wing, working alongside the 'Rank and File' group of EIS in Edinburgh. At Annual General Meetings I regularly seconded what the Establishment called 'daft Midlothian Motions'. These addressed the issues set out above. At that time, I looked like a thoroughly Conservative wifie with my glasses, hair in a bun, camel coat and shiny shoes. I would have spent the night before debate at dinner with Heidies from the North, my home areas, I would have sung and told stories. Given the agenda we worked to, my mind was full of campaigning, and this emerged as songs. From that era came most of my anti-nuclear and anti-war songs. On one occasion I was introduced as 'Anti-Nancy'. At the Heilan Heidies' Dinners I would air these songs. Have no doubt, there is power in a song. If you are campaigning on a matter and you send a letter to the paper they will publish it, but only once. If you deliver an impassioned speech you will get your stage, but only once. However, if you make a song about your concern and it is good enough, you can sing it over and again. I believe that on some occasions I won votes due to the songs I had sung at dinner. These folk, some of them good old-fashioned Scottish Tories, would see me at the podium next morning with the 'Mad Midlothian motions'. They would listen, and vote for me. In that era, Midlothian had great success with motions that had failed in the past. One success was the banning of the belt. I am proud to have seconded that motion. I am sure it passed in part due to the friends I had made in the Social evenings and Song... a great recipe for pure pleasure and for building and developing the fabric of society.

One night, after a union meeting in Edinburgh in 1984, we were watching the news. We saw police horses crash through the picket lines at Hunterston. An Edinburgh friend said, 'Look at those bloody Horses!'.

I, from a croft that worked two Clydesdales, retorted, 'The Horses are not Bloody. They are just doing what they were trained to do'. And, as I considered it, I realised that went for the laddies on their backs too. When I got home I told Denness, son of the Leith docker, 'Aye,' he said, 'some bloody Pit Ponies'.

I sat down, and the words just poured out for 'Maggie's Pit Ponies'.

The Royal Oak Bar

Edinburgh Folk Club led to the Royal Oak.

I liked to enter the annual EFC song-writing competition, and was even lucky enough to win a few. There was another song-writing win I had forgotten until a friend reminded me. It was run by the *Edinburgh Evening News*. (How can a wifie forget something like that? I'll tell you later.) Anyway, I was fortunate enough to win it with 'Listen tae the Teacher'. To celebrate afterwards, Maggie Cruickshank took me along to The Royal Oak, a bar in Infirmary Street. On that merry night this place was brimming with songs and laughter, good company and fun. I could not have imagined then the influence the Oak would have on my life. There I met someone who was to become my best friend and who, like Dot Harcus, was a red-headed woman with a sparkling and powerful personality.

I would defy you to encapsulate Sandra Adams in mere words. Sandra Adams, former White Heather Club dancer, and Creator of the Royal Oak as a singing bar, would need a book to herself – but here's a wee taste.

In 1980, the Royal Oak became the first proper 'singing' pub in Edinburgh. Named for a ship, clinker-built, she breasted the ocean waters of the city-centre with a top-notch crew: Ship's Master, Captain Sandra Adams; First Officer, her Sister Dorothy Taylor; Chief Engineer, Sandra's husband, Peter Stalker. They created somewhere that was a joy to visit with good music, good company and good order.

I went to the Oak to enjoy the evenings Maggie Cruickshank hosted in the downstairs bar. I would sing a song or two, and soon Sandra asked me if I'd host a night. I said I couldn't possibly, I did not have the confidence. 'Of course you can,' she said, 'Sing and play your wee boxie. Be here Sunday night, eight o'clock'. And because of the confidence she clearly had in me, I did, and I loved it.

In the early 1990s, there was major refurbishment of the former Empire Theatre in Nicolson Street, to create the Edinburgh Festival Theatre. The workmen were regular customers of the Oak. When one of them heard I was a songwriter he said, 'Why don't you write a song for us?' So I did. I'm pleased to report that 'The Brickie's Ballad' has had hundreds of outings since then. The vibrant Royal Oak culture was so vital and the folk so interesting that ideas just blossomed. Writing songs was a pleasure

The Oak attracted folk from all over the world and enjoyed music of all kinds, Jazz, Classic, and of course Folk – the very best of each. There was the cream of Folk musicians, both the resident anchor singers and folk who dropped in when on stage in Edinburgh. A number of the Scottish Chamber Orchestra were favourites as violins morphed to fiddles to play a smooth strathspey with cellos and horns. Brian Kellock, the best Jazz Piano player in the world, would pop in, and we have had George Melly and many more at Festival times, all ably accompanied on double bass by Billy Craib of Jim Johnstone's Scottish Dance Band. Here was music in all its multifaceted glory, doing its given duty of bringing people together in good company and true fellowship.

Scottish Chamber Orchestra members would arrive after a gig in the Festival Theatre, sometimes still in white tie and tails, bringing the cast with them. Each year saw a dazzling Christmas musical. One evening this tribe of glammy, sparkly people arrived. Two cellists perched on seat-backs and set to with 'Brochan Lom', perfect for a Highland Schottische. There was a whole square yard of space on the floor. Sandra and I danced that bright, bouncy dance. As we whirled to a halt, one of the company said, 'Hey, ladies, what a purty dance that is. Will you teach me?' 'Nancy will teach you', says Sandra, 'I've to serve'. The young man duly stepped up, and proceeded to make a fine job of the dance. His friends applauded warmly, and he said. 'Gee thanks, that was great. Tell me, what's your name?' 'It's Nancy', I said, 'and who are you?' 'Oh,' he replied, 'I'm Peter ... I'm the dance master for West Side Story.'

Wow, that was some pupil!

Gerda Stevenson and *Hopscotch*

That was the art and the craft of learning in process. As well as the Folk Club and The Royal Oak I regularly attended the Poetry Library and the Saltire Society for events with Norman McCaig, Robert Garioch and others. There, in about 1990, I met Gerda Stevenson, cultural powerhouse of actor, producer, director, writer and singer. She approached me one evening with an intriguing proposal: that I write for *Hopscotch*, a BBC Schools Programme for young ones. I thanked her, but insisted I could not possibly do it. Gerda would not take no for an answer. She tells the story in her piece 'Collaborating with Nancy Nicolson'.

Making the programmes was not the end of the story. There came a day in my teaching life when for various reasons I would call it a day. I had been on placement in the North and returned to my Edinburgh School to gather my gear. I was devastated to be told that the Infant Head had binned all the cassette recordings I had made of the *Hopscotch* programmes as they were broadcast. They were 'out-of-date', she insisted. No word that they had been recorded on cassettes bought with my own money, my own property! I rang Gerda to see about getting copies from the BBC. She duly enquired, only to be informed that BBC Scotland did not archive Schools Programmes! That was us, our programmes and our precious bairns put in our place.

I took my sorry self down to the Oak for comfort. Sandra was brilliant. She appreciated my upset. And as she had done supporting me in previous contretemps with School Management, she gave her verdict. 'They are just jealous, darling. They can't do what you do. They are just jealous!' Well, whether they were jealous or not, it was a great comfort. I still hope against hope that there is a copy somewhere of even a few of these programmes. I am of a mind to publish a collection of Bairns' Songs. These *Hopscotch* programmes contained about eight stories, twenty songs and twenty rhymes. Are there any former infant or nursery teachers out there who hoard things? Do please take a look.

In 1999, The Royal Oak provided a wee brother for the Edinburgh Folk Club. Paddy Bort, now the chair and driving force of EFC, got together with Sandra, Dorothy and Bobby Eaglesham to start 'The Wee Folk Club' as a regular Sunday night folk club in the Downstairs Lounge of the Royal Oak. It's one of my all-time favourite clubs, so cosy and such a great venue for an intimate evening of good music.

Bell's and Hamish Henderson

Good music and congenial company is to be found all around central Edinburgh.

I have some fine friends among the writers of Scotland. One in particular is

Kaitness's own George Gunn, poet, playwright, anarchist and general good lad fey Dunnet. When he came Sooth he was wont to give me a call to meet him in Sandy Bell's, the folk bar in Forrest Road. There, in the '90s, we shared good company, none better than that of Hamish Henderson. From the days when he judged song competitions at Edinburgh Folk Club, Hamish seemed to seep gently into my life. I saw him at concerts and ceilidhs, and always loved to meet him in Bell's along with George. What tunes, what songs, what logic we traded. It was very heaven in a crowded Bell's to be wedged between George and Hamish. I liked the symmetry of HH, GG and NN in good company.

Hamish lived near me, at the edge of the Meadows. I was delighted the first day I met him with Sandy, his dog, right on my own street. I invited him up for coffee and a dram, knowing that I had some Old Pulteney on the shelf. We spoke about Whisky and Bagpipes. With a piper for a Dad I have a head full of pipe-tunes. What a time we had, singin and diddlin tunes. We spoke of the songs Hamish wrote to the pipe tunes that accompanied him as Captain Hamish Henderson in Italy in the Second World War.

Hamish Henderson and Sandy visiting in Nancy's kitchen

'The Freedom Come-Aa-Ye' to 'The Bloody Fields o Flanders' and 'The 51st Highland Division's Farewell To Sicily' to 'Farewell to the Creeks'.

We sang them together. In the course of many visits we spoke at length, but to my sorrow, I can't recall what we spoke of.

Hamish was a great source of strength to me, telling me I was part of Scotland's as well as Edinburgh's cultural life. I do mind he was encouraging me to make another CD of my songs. But, alas, there were those 33 sum books to correct!

I always remember how Hamish greeted me, as he greeted all friends.

I would come in to Bell's. He would see me, stand even taller than usual, tip his head up, spread his arms wide and say in booming tones, 'MY GOD – NANCY!' ... as if I WERE his God. Then he would envelop me in the massive bosom, as fine a place as a wifie might want to be in the middle of doing her Saturday messages!

Flags

Let's stay with Bell's and George Gunn.

In 1996 I had been teaching for 22 years and writing songs for 20 years. Round New Year 1995/96 I wandered into Bell's.

There was George as large as life. The conversation went thus:

GG: Ay, Nancagee, and fit are ye doin in Choon?
NN: A'm teychin Primary 3 in Edinburgh.

GG: No ye're no.
NN: Yes A am.

GG: No, ye're no.
NN: Weel, fit else do ye say A'm doin?

GG: Yu're writin e songs for ma play at Castlehill.
NN: A tell ye A'm no. A canna write til order! And anyway A hev a contract an a class in Edinburgh.

GG: Just ask yer heidie for time off.
NN: A'll no get time off.

GG: Tell im id's a placement, an Arts Placement. Ye'll be workin wi e bairns in Castletoon school.
NN: Oh, id's in a school?

GG: Aye. Id's a school an community project. A play aboot e flagstone industry. Ye'll write songs wi e bairns.
NN: Weel, maybe, maybe if A say A can bring back e skills til use wi ma ain classes.

GG: At's hid. Choost ye ask.

And lo I did ask, and lo it was granted.

I was to spend the whole month of June in Castletown School and village, on the shores of the Pentland Firth, working to make songs, to mentor school bairns and community members in makkin songs, in singing, and making crowd scenes for George's play, *Flags*.

What a welcome I had from Ranald Macauslan, the Heidie. My work was like all the good bits of teaching without all the tiresome bits. I had the run of the school, indulged by Heidie, Teachers and Bairns. We spent time in the airy classrooms, oot in the massive grassy playground, and sometimes away down to the swishing, stoney, historic shore.

The play was to go on in a newly-refurbished steading near Castlehill Quarry. A central character was 'Flaga', the spirit of the flagstones. On the first night the place was packed with folk sitting between the fine flag-stone walls of the building. Lights went down – then the side wall burst open and out leapt Flaga! Folk gasped in astonishment. A sham wall had been created with a gauze and clever lighting. This was what Flaga had burst through. A wee bit of Theatrical Dramatics ... new to me. I loved it.

In my month at Castletoon I learned much of the Flagstone story, and of the workforce, mainly Gaelic-speakers cleared from Sutherland as well as some from Lewis. A key factor of the play was a curse that had been visited on the family of quarry-owner James Traill. 'Flags' was just bursting wi material for makin songs. George needed a key song for Janet, Traill's wife who had dearly wanted a baby. After many years she had a baby boy, but the poor peedie mite died. George has Janet standing alone on the shore, lamenting her lost baby. I made the song 'Cold Comfort'.

But there was a challenge. Heather who played Janet was adamant. She could not sing. She would not sing. She had two sisters who sang like angels and was sure that she could not sing **at all.** 'I'll tell you what we can do', she said, 'you stand behind a screen and sing the song while I mouth the words'. It took me a wee whilie to convince her that this would not do. We sat together, stood and breathed together, spoke together. Gradually I won her trust. We stood facing each other, hands on each others' shoulders and first spoke then hummed songs such as 'Happy Birthday to You' and 'Twinkle Twinkle Little Star'.

Slowly, so slowly, she began to sing. By the time we were done, three weeks later, we had not told folk.

When she went on stage and sang everyone was utterly charmed, none more than me – or maybe Heather herself.

And you, dear reader, are you still sure you canna sing?

I was sorry to leave Castletoon having met so many fascinating folk and learned so much about drama, about the flagstone industry and indeed about myself. I could write songs to order!

Celtic Connections

... which I will call variously Celtic or simply CC when I am being lazy.

I returned to the Edinburgh School for the last few days of term. But it was no longer assumed that I would carry on in there next term. There was a clash of personalities. There was the discovery that my 'Hopscotch' cassettes had been done away with. Things had changed, not least in myself and my expectations of what I wanted to do for the rest of my life. In the summer of 1996 I ceased to be a school-teacher.

For a couple of years I worked at home. I read, I wrote, and I spent time with my family and friends in both Edinburgh and Kaitness. It was good. Then, one morning in 1998 my Edinburgh phone rang at about half past eleven. It was Ranald, the heidie of the Castletown school.

RRR ... RRR ... RRR ... RRR

NN: Hello?
RM: It's Ranald.

NN: Ranald! Should you no be wi Primary 3?
RM: Never mind that: *Times Education Supplement*, page 24, your job!

And, wi a clunk, the phone went down.

So I went oot for the TESS, and the Celtic Connections job *was* mine.

Celtic Connections is a fabulous Festival in Glasgow, created by Colin

Hynd in 1994. Now The Glasgow Royal Concert Hall had won Lottery Funding to create the position of an Education Officer who was to fashion and operate a programme 'to reconnect the children and communities of Glasgow with their Cultural Heritage.'

I was like a pig in the proverbial. Again, as in Castletown, I was able to employ all the fine elements of teaching and none of the bothersome ones. I could give full rein to my knowledge of the Tradition. Colin gave me full access to the entire Celtic Connections bill of artists, the best in the world, to perform concerts at 10 am on weekday mornings in the Main Auditorium of the Concert Hall. The artists revelled in their rapt audience of 2000 bairns, along with the 200 adults, teachers and parents. I loved to sashay on to that great big golden stage and say 'Good Morning' to a full house. John Cairney of the EIS threatened to report me to the Union for taking oversized classes of 2000!

The aim of the programme was to restore the position of Scotland's traditional culture as a natural part of people's lives, not only as an artform, but for what we know to be substantial benefits in individual, social, emotional, intellectual and cultural terms. The target group for concerts was children and young people and I chose to aim for those aged 3-8, the Early Years. The subject was the traditional and indigenous culture of Scotland, its music, song, storytelling and dance. I emphasised that this was to be first and foremost a social and sociable activity rather than 'lessons'. The whole project was built on a pattern of increasing involvement and commitment. We began with the large introductory concerts, then one-off and six-week residency 'Come-and-Try' workshops in school. These were led by established artists, assisted by Glasgow traditional music students from the RSAMD (now Royal Conservatoire of Music) and from the Traditional Music Course of Strathclyde University. These teams delivered specialised teaching through small-group tuition in dance, fiddle, whistle, bodhrán and singing. For a lucky few classes this culminated in an appearance the following January on the same large stage that began the exercise. This allowed me to demonstrate that Art is at the start and heart of learning.

However, I did not possess the expertise to deliver such workshops. But Colin knew someone who did: Caroline Hewat from Inverness.

Caroline wore her skills and talent lightly. She had instituted 'Come And Try' (CAT) workshops at Balnain House in Inverness. These were an inspired learning experience which she helped me put at the very heart of the Celtic Connections Education Programme.

I allocated visits to schools. Caroline told me her method and showed me how to deliver them. I know that many of the assisting students are now in their turn delivering CAT or something similar, and Caroline's work and influence continue to flourish. To date, more than 185,000 children have gone through Celtic Connections workshops. Thank you, Caroline, your influence lives on.

In her own right, Caroline was an outstanding painter, but she always put more effort into getting folk into the arts than in promoting herself and her work. That was the measure of her selflessness.

There was an impressive tribe of Hewats at Celtic Connections. Caroline and her two daughters made a stunning triumvirate of Celtic Creatives. Corrina you may know as the beautiful singer and top clarsach player. In the Education concerts at 10 in the morning she held the bairns entranced. Now, in 2016, she leads and inspires at least one choir and lord knows how many pupils. She has taken on Caroline's mantle, to pass on the tradition. Caroline's other daughter Jade is the lynchpin, the very cornerstone of the administration for the whole CC festival. Many's the time has she saved my artistic and professional life!

With Hewats as partners I could deliver a programme that lived up to the remit I had been charged with.

I was pleased with an assessment of the Education Programme in the *Scottish Education Journal*:

> Clearly the Celtic Connections Education Programnme is very much in tune with recent educational thinking and discussion about the importance of creativity in fostering learning.[1]

Denness: Bad News and Good Years.

---

[1] 'Celtic Connections: Education Programme goes from strength to strength', *The Scottish Educational Journal*, vol.86, no.6 (December 2002), p.13.

Celtic Connections was going great guns. I commuted by train daily to Glasgow. But by 2004-2005 I was aware that Denness was getting thin and peaky. I asked him, then told him, to go to the doctor for a check.

He did not go. I asked again, and again he did not go. It's a thing with men. Do they believe that as long as they dinnae go to the doctor, they cannae be ill? Eventually I reckoned I'd just have to back-neck him down the road myself. It was clear he was seriously unwell. Whatever it was, I'd need to be at home to look after him. I wrote my letter of resignation and handed it to Colin. He threw it back in my face. 'I'm not accepting this', he said. I told him my reason. I had no choice.

The doctor sent Denness for tests, and we went to the Western General Hospital for the results. 'I am sorry to tell you, Mr Morton that you have a cancer of the throat. It is terminal'. These are words that so many have heard. There's the 'Oh, No!' moment, then the great thump to the pit of the stomach, and again 'Oh, No!' But it was definitely, 'Oh, yes'. To win a little more time he was to have two operations.

We got home and sat at the kitchen table. I took his hands in mine. 'Terminal, they said, ... Denness, I'm not giving you permission to die'. Alongside the hospital treatment, I made sure his diet was the best, and that he got rest plus gentle walks in the green air of the Meadows. We would sit in the sunshine that poured in at the kitchen window, listen to the wireless and set the world to rights. Slowly his strength returned. By 2010 he was as well as he had been ten years before. The doctor was astonished. He was delighted to see Denness so well. 'I must admit', he said, 'that at diagnosis we reckoned you would not survive til Christmas'. Denness smiled, 'Nancy wouldn't give me permission to die. I am more afraid of her than of you, so I didn't die.' Science and love together worked that miracle!

Those five years gave us some of the best times we had together. During the frantic years of teaching, Union and gigging, relaxed time together was rare and precious. But even when we had the time, we would be found in our separate spaces, he in the studio, a massive chaotic room, and I in a wee chaotic room at other end of house. We mused on the parallels in our work, our real work, his art and my songwriting. We would engage with the same issues. For two non-believers, we frequently honed in on God. My songs 'The Fairmer' and 'They Sent a Wumman' stand alongside Denness's cartoon of

'Mrs God' to show who really looks after the world. I asked him who 'Mrs God' was based on. He gave me a long look, smiled slowly, and said, 'Who do you think?'

If there is a God, how can he ... or she ... let wars happen? I grant the Bible teaches that he gave us free will. Does that mean he's content to let wicked greedy madmen maim and murder tiny defenceless bairns? Sorry, St Andrew's Sunday School, but I now believe that if there is a God, he's a bastard! No, I am not swearing. He hasna got a faither!

Flowers in the Sand

We were both horrified by Bush and Blair's vicious, self-seeking, murderous actions anent Iraq, and Blair's supposed, invented more like, 'Weapons of Mass Destruction'. I was writing 'Tony B-Liar' and 'Boys and Toys'. Denness was working away in the studio. He said, 'Come and see what you think of this'. It was a massive piece on a sheet of cardboard he had found at the bins opposite our door.

It was stunning – big poppies splashed across a golden ground, with the top right corner cut and slashed. See it on the back cover, look now.

Here is the conversation that ensued:

> **N:** That's wonderful. I love the poppies. What is it?
> **D:** I didnae paint poppies.

> **N:** But I am seeing them there... if not poppies, what is it?
> **D:** It's 'Flowers in the Sand'. 'Flowers in the Sand under a Torn Sky'.

I looked silently for a minute

> **D:** It's the desert sand in Afghanistan and Iraq. The red is blood.
> **N:** Going black in the centre as it dried! But what are the cuts at the top?
> **D:** Air bombardment.
> **N:** But I still see poppies.

> **D:** I didnae paint poppies. The picture is made now. The Picture will tell

you itself what it is.

N: It's telling me poppies!

D: Art in action, Nancy!

I stood back to take in the whole. It was astonishing. Sharply beautiful.

How effectively art can force you to face massive world issues!

So I with my seemingly light, cheeky songs and Denness with his beautiful painting were screaming our anger at the iniquity of War. We frequently used humour, dark, angry humour, to make our arguments. We found a massive sense of commitment and togetherness in this. It was a key bond for us.

Denness died in 2011. I was bereft. Bereft to the extent that I could not organise an obituary for him.

In 2014 we delivered a concert in his honour at that year's Carrying Stream Festival. We used 'Flowers in the Sand' as the backdrop. That was his obituary. It was stunning.

Air Alba

After I had left Celtic Connections in 2005, and when Denness was rallying, getting out and meeting friends, I could put my mind on other things, and fancied doing a gig at the Fringe. It would need more than a list of songs. I'd need a topic (eternal teacher), and thought about Whisky. I was mindin on the grand story of our crofting neighbours who had an illicit still in the Peat Hill for fifteen years, running rings round the Police and Customs. 'Nancy's Whisky' was a one-hour one-woman show. As I worked on it I thought, 'so what about another?' I have plenty songs and opinions about food, Scotland's food, hence 'Oats and Oysters'. And then I did one for Burns, and one for Women. I had a stable of four shows which I presented under the umbrella title of 'Air Alba' – About Scotland – to be staged in the downstairs bar of The Royal Oak.

Sandra, although she had retired from The Royal Oak in 2003, promoted the shows with great energy. Her support and encouragement were brilliant. With ten or more gigs a week we did well. There were quiet days. One afternoon only one man turned up. He grimaced and said, 'I don't suppose you can do the show for one?' I replied, 'Why not? I'm here. You're here. There is nothing to stop us.' It went a treat! Afterwards my grateful audience took me for a wee supper before my evening performance.

If that was my smallest audience, my biggest was a rally for Democracy in the Meadows, with 25,000. I had not been booked, but was near the stage when the organiser found that The McCluskey Brothers were stuck in traffic and could not get there in time. I sang to the masses and got a fabulous response. I canna mind the date, the organisers or the actual title of the gig. If you can tell me I'd be delighted. Why can't I mind? Read on.

Head Dunt

In 2009, I had a wee adventure that quite upturned my life. During Celtic Connections I had taken a break to see a Mozart Oratorio at Glasgow City Halls. It was scintillating. Afterwards I was enjoying a glass of wine in a smart bar nearby when a man I did not know took it into his head to assault me. He lunged at me, struck me on both shoulders with all his power and sent me reeling backwards. I managed a few neat Shetland back-steps, but still fell backwards onto my head on the hard floor.

I've had an interesting time since then, with long- and short-term memory problems, with face-blindness (inability to recognise the face even of someone I'd been talking to the day before). There were many lost skills such as prioritising, sequencing and organising, just the skills I would need to write a book or plan a concert! Life is such fun with half a head! I lose things, buy several of the same items, tell folk the same thing ten times over, but forget to tell them the one urgent, important thing they really need to know. I have the greatest difficulty making a shopping list or packing a suitcase. I did recently pack a case with three toothbrushes and no knickers! However, family and friends have been such treasures that I still get by. I do appear more ditzy than formerly, but folk don't seem to mind too much. Maybe they don't see any difference.

Togetherness: His-and-Her Cancers

In spring 2011 I had my annual breast scan. Denness had a test scan of his throat. We were both due to get the results at the Western General on the very same morning! Each chummed the other to their report. We both needed similar operations! What are the odds against that? I reckon that if I had written it in a story script the editor would have thrown it back at me! My operation went fine, and the cancer is clear. Denness's went fine until a nasty little blood clot lodged in his lung, and took away my wonderful man.

How far away do folk go when they die? I am not superstitious – well, not much. I do not believe that folk exist in another form after death.

So why do I keep 'seeing Denness' every time a guy with white hair and a donkey jacket walks round a corner?

Why, when I see something interesting do I catch myself thinking, 'I must tell Denness'? – And why do I take photos of things to 'show Denness'?

I am sure that I am not the only person visited by such thoughts.

Lifting the Bad Spell

January 2016 marked seven years since the assault. In that time I believe I have created a reasonably convincing illusion of being a whole person. There are many ways of getting by, especially with the support of Family and Friends. The injury is responsible for a now lost world, but I have found ways to make a new world.

In stories, the wee heroine may be put under a bad spell. Bad spells don't last forever. They end after seven years when she kisses a frog or some such. Well, I didn't kiss a frog, but I have been living a fresh new life. I admit that means taking on more than I can cope with, but I did that before the dunt. That's Life. And life for me now is doing things I never imagined I would do.

The Book. This Book or None!

The most recent surprise is that I have written a book.

'How?' I ask myself. Here's how.

In early 2016, I stepped into Bell's and there was George Gunn.

He folds me in an enormous cuddle and is saying something into my hair. 'At's great aboot e concert, and e book laanch on e same nicht!' So George has written another book? I step back and ask, 'Fit concert? Fit Book?' 'Yur Concert,' he says, 'Yur concert an yur book. Id is iss year yu're 75? Paddy Bort is doin id, for yur birthday'. And that was the first I had heard of it.

But if Paddy Bort says you are writing a book, you write a book.

It is being finished at the very last minute.

My daughter Janet suggested we call it 'They Sent A Wumman … at the Last Minute'.

Where, I wonder, did she learn such impertinence?

I have tried not to tell you any lies. However, with my broken head that's quite difficult. If you see anything I got wrong, DO get in touch to correct it for me.[2] However, dear reader, the choice was not between doing a flawed book or a best book; it was between doing this book or no book at all!

I truly hope that as you read, the stories triggered thoughts and memories of your own life. Gather them together. You'll need them to write your book. Reflect on your own potential. There's so much in you that needs to come to the surface not only for your own sake and for those dear to you, but maybe for the delectation of Scotland and the World. And no, I'm no jokin!!

I would never have had such a pleasant and enjoyable life without the folk who saw in me what I refused myself to see, and who encouraged me to find myself.

Take your bow, Sandra Adams, George Gunn, Hamish Henderson, Colin Hynd, Ewan McVicar, Gerda Stevenson, and many more. I look on you as my pushers, proper and welcome pushers.

And Bairns Again

Here, we are nearly at the end, but before I go I want to share my all-time favourite example of bairns making sense of language. I have always liked Christmas songs and Carols. One of the loveliest is 'Away in a Manger'. As a peedie lassie I had worked out what a manger was, but never quite understood the use of the word 'away' in the first line. In what sense was Jesus 'away'? Surely he was right there! OK, Bethlehem was far away, but the first line never totally worked for me. I dismissed it as just another adult oddity.

As Celtic Connections Education Officer I loved to visit Glasgow Schools, especially around Christmas. In a Primary One class I began to sing 'Away in a Manger'. The bairns joined in, 'Lovely,' I thought. But what was that they were singing? It was different. I listened carefully. I watched their lips. They were singing, 'A **Wean** in a Manger'!

---

[2] You can email me: <nancynicolson@btinternet.com>

The bairns with their fresh original thinking had expressed the Nativity to perfection, for isn't that precisely what the Holy Infant was?

A WEAN in a Manger!

Trust the children. Trust the bairns. Trust the WEANS.

Now read on and SING!

Nancy and the Bard (statue of Robert Burns by Jan Miller, owned by Pete Heywood)

FLITTING IN A HEN HOOSE:

The Songs of Nancy Nicolson

George Gunn

Anton Chekhov once told Maxim Gorky that he had a dream to build a sanatorium for sick teachers in the village of Kuchuk-Koi where he was living. It would be a building full of light with big windows and high ceilings. It would have a splendid library with all sorts of musical instruments, an apiary, a vegetable garden and an orchard.

"I'd have lectures on agronomy, meteorology, and so on – teachers ought to know everything, old man, everything."

Chekhov then coughed, smiled at Gorky and said,

"The teacher must be an actor, an artist, passionately in love with his work, and our teachers are navvies, half educated individuals, who go to the village to teach children as willingly as they would go to exile."

In his short life of 44 years, Chekhov built several schools but he was never to realise his dream of a teachers' sanatorium. He would, I am willing to bet, approve of the songs of Nancy Nicolson which, although forged in a Caithness cultural smiddy, were born out of her 30 years as a primary school teacher and EIS activist. Anyone who has heard her songs from the 1990 collection, *Rhyme and Reason* or, even better, seen her perform them live will realise at once that here is a woman "passionately in love with *her* work", as Chekhov demanded. Yet here is an artist who also understands the world and circumstances of the 'navvy' and the 'exile' as well as the consequences of a possible nuclear Armageddon, which must be (has to be) countered by the limitless beauty of a child's imagination if humanity is to have any future.

Recently Nancy and I sat in a Wick pub chewing optimistic lettuce and pessimistic chicken, drinking budget-price white wine and enjoying the long Summer light as it bounced endlessly off Market Square in June and she told me.

"In schools what I want to do is to convince the teachers and parents that this (song writing) is not a fringe on the edge of Life, and get loose on them and demonstrate that stories and songs and stuff are marks of awareness and that it can build up skills and how all that enriches communities."

From her song writing debut in 1975, (she was 33 years old – "I was a late starter," she says) coming second with 'Granda Said' to Sheila Douglas in a competition judged by Alistair Clark and Hamish Henderson, Nancy Nicolson has continued, through her songs, to "get loose" not just on schools but on the broad fabric of Scottish cultural life. This, arguably, reached its organisational apex when she was appointed in 1998 as Education Officer for the Celtic Connections music festival in Glasgow, based in the Royal Concert Hall, a post she held for six years. Now, at 75, she has entered that period in her life where 'struggle' has made the transition into 'achievement', but it was a long and, at times, a rocky road.

Travelling into an uncertain, unknowable future on rickety vehicles, songs being some of the more robust transportation she has employed as we shall see, has always been the style of Nancy Nicolson. The poet Norman MacCaig once remarked that he saw no reason why "Scotland can't go to Hell on her own hand cart"; so it has been for this Caithness song-smith, from her very beginnings to her 75th year. It is a journey all of Scotland should celebrate. The unfortunate reality is that the songs of Nancy Nicolson are not better known, which is indicative of both the nascent and repressed state of cultural and expressive life in this country, especially (and ironically) in schools.

Nancy Nicolson was born on 10 November 1941 in a farm cottage at Toftcarl, at Hempriggs just south of Wick, which was where her father Bill worked. These were the darkest days of World War Two. The previous October the final phase of the German attack on Russia began and the first of the Arctic convoys to offer the Soviets some aid began their perilous voyages through the ice and enemy fire to Archangelsk and Murmansk. In December the Japanese attacked Pearl Harbour. Britain and America declare war on Japan and days afterwards Germany declares war on America. In Wick itself Coastal Command had established a huge airfield and the sound of Spitfires and Hurricanes daily filled the huge Caithness sky. All things being equal, Bill and Betty Nicolson having a child in the Winter of 1941 was either an act of supreme folly or of supreme optimism. However, despite the desperate geo-political situation and the destructive march of fascism, optimism was to prevail. Human energy must find its form. In 1941 Neil Gunn published his magnum opus, *The Silver Darlings*, the third in his historic trilogy of novels, and put Caithness at the centre of Scottish literature. War and imagination have a tendency to transfer the edge and the liminal to the centre of focus. Struggle changes perception. As 1941 blew itself to a conclusion Gunn was writing *Young Art and Old Hector* and by the time 1945 came along he had published five books, including his most dystopian and futuristic novel, *The Green Isle of the Great Deep*, in 1944.

As 1945 saw the world make the transition from war to peace it also saw the four-year-old 'Nancy' Anne Hamilton Nicolson move with her family from the cottage at Toftcarl to her Grandfather's croft at Newtonhill a mile West of Wick.

"We flitted in a henhouse!" she tells me, the memory stirring mischief in her eyes. "My faither put railway sleepers under this henhouse. Here wis hen boxes put in and then things lek mattresses, boxes and ither belongings and then me. He yoked the horse to it, and off we went!"

An unusual method of conveyance by conventional standards, but normal for war traumatised Caithness and yet, on the other hand, it was just another typical example of croft engineering. In such a rural society invention is survival. With this in mind I asked her, since she was Christened Anne, how she came by the name Nancy?

"Weel, the Hamilton was the maiden name o my Nicolson granny who died before I was born. When I wis still a six month ould bairn at Toftcarl a cousin wis born til my dad's sister. She wis also called Anne Hamilton. Ma Granda (Sanny) Stewart, my mither's faither who wis a herrin fisherman fae Sarclet afore hae worked ay ferm, foresaw a difficulty. 'Wae'll hev til do something or fowk'll call them beeg Anne or peedie Anne, or black Anne or white Anne. Ah think wae'll call wur ain Nancy!'"

She laughs as she tells this story. Comedy, after all, is full of people being other people. Here she is before me, Nancy the storyteller.

"I think of the derivation as Anne-Nan-Nancy! It was appropriate too as the Gran Hamilton I was named after was also called Nan Hamilton. I choost love bein Nancy!"

The strange vehicles of transition started even earlier than the flit in a hen-hoose. Nancy is warming to her theme.

"When I was two, Granda Sanny Stewart got a peedie barrow made for me by the prisoners-o-war at Watten. It was green wae 'Nancy' painted on each side. I transported endless loads all over ay place!"

So, as war raged across Europe, play broke out all over Toftcarl. "Playing is a bairn's work," she informs me. I feel Chekhov's shade enter the former Post Office posing as a bar and joining us at our table. The Sunlight bounces off the Market Square cobbles. In any other country we would be sitting outside comfortable in the café culture born out of the climate, but this is Wick, and the Caithness climate is steeped too deep into the collective memory of both of us: we know better. We stay put with the spirit of Chekhov, our wilting lettuce and pale, half-chewed chicken fillets. We sip our wine. I ask her about Caithness and about what it means to her.

"How important is your mother?" Nancy replies. "It's bones, blood and flesh: that's Caithness."

I ask how this translates into her songs. "Well," she says, thinking for a moment, "Comin from ay North we see things from this perspective. We know what we see isna universal. We're good at seein things wae fresh eyes and takin a wicked pleasure in it. Its crofting in songs! It's to look at things from first principles. To have vitality!"

Both Chekhov's shade and I nod in agreement. "There is always Caithness voices in my head. Ye hev a responsibility to the ground beneath yer feet."

One thing Nancy and I agree on and lament upon (Chekhov has his own problems) is that to most Scots Caithness is an unknown place. When they think about it at all it is either as a vague bit North of the Highlands or somewhere you must go if you want to go to Orkney.

"Everything North of Inverness is not the Highlands," Nancy informs anyone who will listen. "I can be quite boring about this!"

So just what is Caithness, this place we both love so much? This is what Neil Gunn had to say about the place in an essay entitled 'Caithness and Sutherland' which was published in *Scottish Country* in 1935:

> From that background, or as it were from that door (he's looking
> back North from the top of the Strath of Kildonan) you walk out

upon Caithness, and at once experience an austerity in the flat clean wind-swept lands that affects the mind almost with a sense of shock. There is something more in it than contrast. It is a movement of the spirit that finds in the austerity, because strength is there also, a final serenity. I know of no other landscape in Scotland that achieves this harmony, that, in the very moment of purging the mind of its dramatic grandeur, leaves it free and ennobled. The Pentland Firth, outreaching on the left, is of a blueness that I, at least, failed to find in the Mediterranean; a living blueness, cold-glittering in the Sun and smashed to gleaming snowdrift on the bows of the great rock-battleships of the Orkneys, bare and austere also. The wind of time has searched out even the flaws here and cleansed them.

So, "free and ennobled", in 1960 an eighteen-year-old Nancy Nicolson left the Caithness croft in Newtonhill and went to Edinburgh and to University. Here was the world of song she subconsciously had been looking for. By 1962, accompanied by her Orkney pal Dot Harcus in Edinburgh's student pubs and in the Crown Bar and at the Blues Club she met such influential characters as Archie Fisher, Owen Hand, Bert Jansch and Clive Palmer.

"To hev a song. A song to be sung. A song that does its job. That was what I craved. But I was shy. Id took weeks and weeks to pluck up the courage to sing at the Edinburgh Folk Club. I'd sung in pubs and at New Year and at school. My development was parallel to the Folk Revival but I didna really know what id wis. I mind askin at ay time, 'Fits folk music?'. Id wis all iss ould songs an ould tunes. But at the same time id was something new. Folk clubs and their repertoire were important because they were where I became confident in my own voice."

Self-confidence is difficult to acquire when the knowledge of your own culture has been denied you and you do not have the level of expectancy to rule the world which is the norm of the Oxbridge elite who still, sadly, dominate the arts and manage the perception of what the arts are in Scotland. If we cannot, as Scots, run our own arts organisations, how can we expect to run our own country?

Nancy looks out of the window at the sunlight as if to draw strength. I look at Chekhov's shade as if to borrow money.

"My faither, Bill Nicolson, wis a piper and a founder member of the Wick Pipe Band. Dad playin ay pipes wis what helped put me to sleep an he wis ay best ditch deeger in East Caithness!" and Nancy laughs out loud again, like a burn running into a lochan.

"The things wae held dear in oor family were bands and music and yet I couldna sing at ay Caithness Music Festival for example. Although I mind when I was twelve years ould I learned that I enjoyed addressing an audience. Id was in St Andrews Kirk in Argyll Square in Wick. Readin ay lesson from a beeg book on a lectern. Total silence. My own voice coman back to me. Id wis only much later on I really discovered I could sing when I wis workin wae Primary Two, knowin that I widna be criticised."

This woman, sitting so bonny and brave across the table from me in this Wick pub, like all creative artists has to slide on the razor's edge of self-confidence and self-doubt and like every artist before her she gets cut as a result. Even the choice of what course to follow at Edinburgh University was fraught with what was expected and what was desired, the dichotomy of the time.

"For some strange reason I went to University to study Pure Maths, Physics, Chemistry. Since this was a science degree rather than an arts degree, I was put in classes called 'second ordinary maths' and 'second ordinary natural philosophy' that is 'physics' to you and me. These were essentially second year courses, assuming entrants had done extra years advanced study at school. I had not. I failed miserably. I was mortified. Ashamed of letting family down, utterly sunk! Had I been following any kind of arts degree I would have been in the 'first ordinary' class in each discipline. Why was I in for a science degree?"

The air hangs silent as the answer forms in the June sunlight pouring in the pub door as some Wickers come and go. Chekhov's shade leans over to me and whispers the answer in my ear. At the same time Nancy continues, answering her own question and, unknowingly, agreeing with our invisible Russian guest,

"Dounreay. Because at the time Dounreay and the schools were *pushing* folk into science, especially keen to get girls, and to do science related to nuclear industry, then brand new in Caithness. Ye ken me, – I should've been in

Arts. But in those days I was a good girl. Ah did fit Ah wis telt! So what to do to save my broken self? I felt I had to move to a course I could not possibly fail. I was the most awful traitor til masel. I had to go for the only job in the world I knew I *didna* want til do. I went to Moray House Teacher Training College. That was how strong was my sense of duty to Mam and Dad... no til disgrace them again."

There is no lettuce left; the chicken and the wine along with Chekhov's shade have all disappeared. Nancy Nicolson, as usual, notices everything. She goes on, "I still admire, respect, even love the disciplines of maths and physics. They can be pure music, pure magic. But now that I've said all that I wonder if at least *some* of my anti-Dounreay feelings are rooted way back then?"

Even as we speak, poet to singer, some twenty-five miles away on the North coast of Caithness, the decommissioning of Dounreay proceeds at a snail's pace. What was once the white heat of the technological revolution, forged in the time of Dan Dare and Sputnik, in the depths of the Cold War and the attendant institutionalised paranoia, now is literally tons of radioactive rust. The Nuclear Decommissioning Authority is about to spend £8 million upgrading the runway at Wick Airport so that they can transport dodgy uranium and other nuclear stuff across to the United States who filched it in the first place from several imploding former Soviet republics in the nineteen nineties. No other state but Britain would accept this weapons grade junk and of course the only 'safe place' to store it was Dounreay. Naturally. They can decommission the nuclear plant but they are having difficulty decommissioning the people: they are expected to fend for themselves. The nuclear waste at Dounreay will be buried beneath the ground next door to the site at Buldoo, while the residual atomic population walk the streets of Thurso (Atomic City) trying to find a future. Meanwhile 'exotic' nuclear waste (Uranium, plutonium and radioactive sodium) leaves Caithness every week by road, rail and sea. The people tend to disappear like Chekhov's ghost. The total cost of decommissioning Dounreay is conservatively estimated at £2.9 billion. The amount spent on the people, so far, has been minimal.

These realities are what inform Nancy Nicolson's witty yet visceral song 'E Man at Muffed Id'. So I ask her how she goes about writing a song. She seems surprised that I should be foolish enough to ask such a question.

"I have no method or process, if at's what ye mean?" she says. "Language triggers words. Stories are sources. Id's all a fusion o sound, words an wit. Oh an love an music. Life, Cheorge, life!"

Feeling a bit foolish I press on and ask something equally stupid. Where is that damned Russian ghost when you need him? Nancy smiles, sensing my difficulty.

"I want ma songs til be tall and strong in Caithness Scots. Life is yer song material. I mind when I wis aboot fower and wae hed iss pair oh workin Clydesdales an I wid water them. From that came 'Maggie's Pit Ponies' an 'Horsagee, The Heilan Horse'. I try and find a narrative voice. I write what comes intil my heid."

For those who do not know the songs of Nancy Nicolson it would be fair to say, by way of introduction, that they are deceptively simple. Behind this structural invitation, which manages to be both deceptive and gentle, are songs that the critic Alistair Clark has called "cunningly temperate". Very few songwriters could bring off a song about the nuclear stand-off between the world's two super powers in the form of a nursery rhyme, which is exactly what Nancy Nicolson achieves in 'The Eagle and The Bear'. Contrast that to the almost Bach-like quality of 'Last Carol' with its beautiful cascades of lyrics about "mushroom cloud and heavy water" and "nuclear fission". Add to this the heart breaking balladry of 'Who Pays the Piper', a searingly beautiful, angry and sad song about the Piper Alpha disaster in the North Sea in 1988 when 167 men were murdered by Occidental Oil.

For all their social awareness and political acumen, their dialectic of justice and their essential human demand for truth, these are most definitely songs from an inclusive feminine consciousness. Sometimes, as in 'The Mistress', this is mixed with an affecting other-worldliness which is haunting but never fey. Nancy Nicolson is not a sentimental song writer. Sometimes wit is the lever employed to open out the meaning of a song, which is used to great effect in 'Don't Call Maggie a Cat'.

In the new world of post-feminism such things may be self-evident, or arguably not. Coming from a 1950s Caithness crofting community was in reality, to get to here in the early decades of the twenty-first century, like stepping out of the nineteenth century. The poet Edwin Muir describes a similar experience in his autobiography of 1940, *The Story and The Fable*, where he describes arriving in an industrial early twentieth-century Glasgow from an eighteenth-century Orkney. In his 1934 novel of the Highland Clearances, *Butcher's Broom*, Neil Gunn has this to say of such a society,

> The women were the more persistent and fruitful workers, and found the males frequently in their way. Many of the tasks about the house they would not let a man perform – even if he had wanted to, which, of course, he did not... The system worked very well, for the man in his sphere and the women in hers were each equally governing and indispensable.

The society Neil Gunn described was a social matrix under severe pressure: clearance, war, starvation and emigration. In the late nineteen-fifties and early sixties the people of Caithness were also under pressure to either accept the nuclear orthodoxy or find another way to live, which usually implied leaving. To survive the pressure of the evictions of Butcher's Broom or the anti-democratic nuclear reality of Dounreay requires great determination. This quality, as possessed by her ancestors, Nancy Nicolson displays in her songs. These are not psycho-dramas concerning the traumas of an internal world. Rather they are ballads and hymns of the everyday experience of characters who have to deal with the daily crises life presents them with. They are not romantic and they are far from rustic. Their form often betrays their content. For example, in 'The Lesson', Nancy Nicolson employs straight-forward story telling in order to say what she has to say about language, education and morality. This is song as pure story.

As to song writing in general she has this to say.

"My tunes are like life tunes and I write what comes into my head. I may not be absolutely sure where a lyric comes from but on the other hand I know when a song is finished. Robert Burns was a great influence. His mission was to save songs. I recognised in Burns things that were important and true. His values were international and he was a citizen of the world."

All art, of course, comes at a cost. Burns, the saviour of Scottish song, was dead at 37. Anton Chekhov, the great generous and open heart of Russian literature (and our friendly ghost), as has been already stated, was dead at 44. Who indeed pays the piper?

I have known Nancy Nicolson for almost forty years. I have watched her grow in both confidence and stature as a songwriter, as an artist. I have watched her struggle to find her voice, and on finding it I have been fascinated to see how that voice has developed. It is not just the singing voice because that has always possessed that quality the travelling people call 'conyach', which is related, or at least Hamish Henderson thought so, to the Gaelic 'caoineadh' or 'weeping', from which we get the word 'keening'. This wordless 'conyach' can be found in her own recorded versions of her own songs, 'Last Carol' and 'Who Pays the Piper?' which are on the CD *Rhyme and Reason*. The other voice, of course, is the political voice. This can be surprisingly and refreshingly angry.

Her song 'Maggie's Pit Ponies' was born and found its feet during the bitter miners' strike of 1984-5. During that troubled time Nancy Nicolson worked in a Lothian school which was not far away from Bilston Glen and Monktonhall, the two pits which saw some savage police actions in order to allow strike-breaking lorries in and out of the site gates and to break up secondary picketing. The violence and heartache which this strike caused – and it was brought about in the first instance and caused by a Tory government determined to shut coal mines as a tactic in a class war – is difficult for those who did not live through it to understand. For the best part of two years Scotland was both an occupied country and a country in conflict. Yorkshire and Metropolitan police officers were drafted in, along with soldiers in police uniforms, to surround the coalmines and manhandle and beat the striking miners when it suited them, all the time waving their overtime payslips in their faces. I remember going down to Ayrshire to perform at a benefit for the striking miners there and the car I was in being followed all the way from Glasgow by a police vehicle – the venue had to be changed three times so that the police could not shut it down and we eventually performed in the social club of Auchinleck junior football club – and then we were followed all the way back to Glasgow. The families of the miners in Ayrshire, close to Christmas in 1984, were surviving on food sent over in a container by the Miners' Union of the Soviet Union. I remember doing countless benefits for the National Union of Mineworkers with Nancy Nicolson and many other committed folk singers and musicians. I must have heard 'Maggie's Pit Ponies' a hundred times. Yet now, 31 years later, I can still hear Nancy singing the lines,

> *Here come the cavalry*
> *here come the troops*
> *here come Maggie's pit ponies*

At a time when the security services in Britain were out of control – the anti-nuclear campaigners Hilda Murrell and Willie MacRae were both murdered in 1984 and 1985 respectively – here was a singer who was totally in control of her art, who took a mature, poetic and insightful look at just what was going on. 'Maggie's Pit Ponies' is a work of powerful observation. It is, I think, one of the best songs to come out of the Miners' Strike. Where other songwriters engaged in rage against the democratic deficit still current in Scotland's relationship with the UK (the recent EU referendum being the latest example) and the blatant political impositions of Thatcher's regime, Nancy Nicolson's political anger was channelled through wit and the quiet passion of observation. 'Maggie's Pit Ponies' is a record of the times, a slice of history as much as it is a song, an acoustic document of humanity.

Likewise, does 'E Man at Muffed Id' employ the technique of dispassionate observation, but this time the anger engendered by the Miners' Strike is replaced by humour and a lightness of touch. This is one of her most assured compositions. The result is none-the-less equally revealing and the moral message of the song is positively scathing. 'Muff', as in "muffed id", refers to United Kingdom Atomic Energy Authority jargon for 'materials unaccounted for' or,

> I'm e man at muffed id
> *I'm e man at boobed*
> *I'm e man at lost e radioactive tube.*

The song, which is a litany of situations where the "radioactive tube" could be – in a lobster creel, a whisky still, on a croft – disguises the tragedy of where it actually is and what that means environmentally, and it also posits the age-old conundrum: is a thing lost if you know where it is? The comedy leads the listener into the black reality of the nuclear industry where everyone who works in it has signed the Official Secrets Act, robbing them of their civil rights, thus rendering a significant percentage of the population of Caithness silent, unable to tell the truth. The truth being that Dounreay, like all nuclear facilities in Britain, is a military installation. During the Cold War the icy reality was that if Dounreay was taken out in a Soviet attack – it was a Level Two target – the population of Caithness and Sutherland would be considered military casualties and would not appear on any civil list, supposing that there was anyone left alive to compose or read such a list.

'E Man at Muffed Id' gets to the heart of the nuclear nightmare like no other song written because it is written from the inside of the bad dream, by a native. Only Nancy Nicolson could have written it. Her gift is that she keeps her indignation, her justified anger, tender and constantly on the move: the anger is never allowed to settle. In this song the singing voice meets the political voice in a chilling splice. The song is subversive because it speaks for all those who are gagged by the Official Secrets Act and 60 years of nuclear industry behavioural conditioning in a society where, as a result, truth is replaced by rumour and the slogan "whatever you say, say nothing" is tattooed onto the consciousness of generations. I remember her singing it at the Northlands Festival in Caithness, which was an arts festival put on to provide "real" culture to the upper echelons of Caithness society. Ferelith Lean had asked me to organise two 'local' concerts of 'local' culture, which I did. After the second one we were in the Thurso Club on Janet Street (the Festival Club) rather late one night and it was full of Dounreay middle and senior management and the upper echelons of Caithness society. Nancy started to sing "A'm e man at muffed id, A'm the man at boobed..." – and there was a strange silence which fell over the place and, as she proceeded with the song, the Dounreay lot and the local toffs sort of shuffled away from her to the far corners of the room as if they had been shown a voodoo sign. It was like the parting of the Red Sea. I thought, at the time, of T.S. Eliot's pessimistic line from 'The Four Quartets', "Humankind cannot bear very much reality", or from 'The Waste Land', "I did not think that death had undone so many."

Reality, however, was the name of the game in 1998 when Nancy Nicolson became the Education Officer for Celtic Connections, and life was there for the living. It was "a major thing in my life" she tells me. "Full stop!" I asked her why, exactly?

"It came at the right time because I had left education efter a stushie wae the headie in 1996. It wis a bad experience. Then I saw the job advertised in the *Times Ed Scotland*, or rather I wis telt aboot id by a freend. I'm such a dreamer. I always believe ay magical thing can happen! Anyway, I got ay chob so I had til establish an educational programme for Celtic Connections during the festival and also a yearlong programme wae schools. It wis heaven. In schools ye were always stopped from doin this kinda work. Celtic Connections wis the opposite. Colin Hynd, head of Celtic Connections, informed me that at interview I had totally undersold masel. On my first day he said to me, 'You tell me what you want to do. YOU're the boss. You know about education and the folk world.' But it wisna helicopter visits to schools. It was the same musicians over 6 weeks til a school and concerts during the festival in the main concert hall. I think id wis the first one where the stage manager had to push me onto the stage. But stepping out on that stage I knew, this is where I need to be."

I watch her expectantly as her eyes wander somewhere above my head, as if she is searching for that moment to return. Then she's off again,

"An audience of 2000, from nursery to Primary 7. There wis nobody between me and the bairns. There was such a response and warmth for six years. But by 2005 Denness (her late husband Denness Morton) was so ill."

Tragically Denness died in 2011, which was one of the roughest bumps on the journey for Nancy Nicolson. But if your first major journey in life is undertaken in a henhoose then you are prepared, more or less, to deal with whatever life throws your way. There were other rough times. In 2009 Nancy was the innocent bystander in a pub brawl and as a result she was knocked over and injured her head: "E dunt on e heid," as she calls it. The result was severe memory problems, amongst other complications. What it meant in artistic terms is that she did not write for three years. This was a crisis in creativity. I ask her how she overcame it? How did she get back?

"It was difficult. My motivation wis low and soon I wis livin on my own. I wis diminished as a human but some good things came oot oh id. I began til appreciate ay real things in life: family, friends, things that really matter. At no time did I think I wis no goin til write or perform. Although I thought there wid come a time or situation when nobody will know me. Now after seven years I thocht, uch, that's enough. I'm very glad that the creative thing has never left me. I still canna pack a suitcase or write a shoppin list, but I'm gled id's that way aroond."

It cannot be stressed enough what a dangerous time this was for Nancy

Nicolson. Those of us who knew and loved her were fearful that we would lose her, and that thought was too terrible to contemplate. To see her back on the stage at the Scottish Storytelling Centre in 2014 in a concert to mark the life of her husband Denness Morton, surrounded by the best of Scotland's folk musicians and singers, was to realise that there is something indomitable about her, a tender robustness that no wee nyaff in a pub or headie in a school can destroy. It has made her stronger.

As she has grown older her Caithness roots, which she has never forgotten and has constantly drawn on, have become to mean even more to Nancy Nicolson. This presents the opportunity to ask: just where do the songs of Nancy Nicolson actually come from? Maybe the innocent question asked by a 18-year-old student in 1960 Edinburgh still has purchase: "Fits folk music?" In Caithness cultural terms this is an important question, especially in relation to song. In Caithness there is a strong tradition of pipe music and of fiddling. Nancy's father was a piper, for example, as were my own uncles. One of the best fiddlers in Scottish folk music at the moment is Gordon Gunn from Wick, but there is no folk song tradition, or at least not one that has survived. The rich oral culture that sustained the Caithness people prior to the "improvements" of the 1770s when land was enclosed by Sir John Sinclair of Ulbster and Dunbar of Hempriggs and the landless cottars, many of whom were Gaelic speaking, were cleared to the poor coastal districts, was lost. The resultant big square fields of nineteenth century Caithness (the "big fields of war" as I call them) bred a cap-doffing peasantry who were encouraged to abandon all traces of their indigenous culture either through the teachings of the Church of Scotland or by law. This cultural denial was also practised by the United Kingdom Atomic Energy Authority in Caithness from the 1950s to the present and is now, sadly, carried on by the people themselves. 'Real culture', as promoted by the Northlands Festival – classical and Anglo-German – was what we were instructed to 'aspire' to. Our own language and culture would only keep us back. Progress was to be a process of denying who we were.

This history of denial is a common theme running through the songs of Nancy Nicolson. In fact, one could question if they are, strictly, folk songs at all? The perennial debate about just what constitutes a 'folk song' is both ultimately as pointless as it is misguided. Legend has it that Big Bill Broonzy was being interviewed on radio by Studs Terkel and after he had sung a song Terkel asked him, "Is that a folk song?" Broonzy replied, "I ain't never heard no horses sing it." To Big Bill Broonzy all music was 'folk music'. Yet there is something radiantly un-folky about Nancy Nicolson's songs and, although she does come from a general Scottish folk tradition, her songs have echoes of a more fluid world of music hall crossed with certain 'front of curtain' numbers from 'Five Past Eight Shows' at the Glasgow Alhambra in the 1950s and 60s. Throw in a good smattering of political protest, as in the songs of Joe Hill, and radical proletarian hymns of the International Workers of the World (the Wobblies), with an infusion of The White Heather Club and Hootenanny from 1960s black and white TV, and the result is songs from popular culture: the songs of Nancy Nicolson. To pull all these strands together, to create a distinctive voice, and to do so consistently in the face of adversity for over forty years, is the mark of a mature artist. The ultimate irony is that in being a generalist, as in her myriad influences, she has carved a unique territory for herself within the canon of Scottish song. She has done what all real artists do: she has preserved a tradition and, especially in Caithness song writing, created a tradition. It is the singers of the future who will benefit.

The afternoon in the converted Post Office which serves as a pub in Wick draws on. The plates have long been uplifted and taken away. Our glasses are empty. The clear June light still dances across the Market Square cobbles. I hear the invasive "pop-pop-clap" of Wimbledon coming from the TV. I notice that Chekhov's shade has returned. Maybe he forgot his ghostly hat? Without warning Nancy says, as she gathers up her bag and stuff to go,

"I'm booking a place at the teachers' sanatorium *now*. Funded by EIS!"

She laughs. Chekhov's shade laughs. He picks up his invisible hat and leaves a happy spirit. He now has at least one recruit. Nancy and I embrace. She leaves, humming a tune to herself as she walks out into the sunlight. I look out of the window, half expecting to see a henhoose waiting for her. Off she goes, her songs following her like fulmars gliding on the wind.

COLLABORATING WITH NANCY NICOLSON

Gerda Stevenson

Before I ever met Nancy Nicolson, I was mesmerised by her abilities as a singer/songwriter and storyteller. I often saw her performing at poetry readings and ceilidhs, and was in awe (still am!) of her quiet power. Her wit is irresistible – that deft way she has of undermining pompousness and political injustice, often with delicious humour. She gets up onto the stage without any fuss, sometimes with her accordion, sometimes just herself with no accompaniment, and starts chatting to the audience as if she's known us all her life, a neighbour dropping in for a bit of crack. Then, as part of the chat, her songs emerge as an extension of speech, utterly natural, often with a short la-la-la phrase sung gently before slipping into a song. Her voice has a lovely lightness and perfect clarity, the subtle words and all their inventive rhyming structures ringing with her distinctly Caithness tones.

The first of Nancy's songs I fell in love with was 'The Mistress', a hauntingly beautiful ballad about the sea:

> *Her eyes are dark, her breast is deep,*
> *That steals a wedded woman's sleep,*
> *That tempts good men into her keep,*
> *And will not let them free,*
> *The moon upon her shoulder gleams,*
> *That siren of the ocean streams,*
> *That whispers in a seaman's dreams,*
> *"No mistress have but me".*

I bought a recording of Nancy's songs, *Rhyme & Reason*, produced on cassette in 1990. ('The Mistress' is the second of seventeen tracks.) At that time I was working as a free-lance radio producer for BBC Scotland's Radio Education department. One of the existing series I was put in charge of was *Hopscotch*, created for nursery and early primary school children. Each programme had a simple 15 minute structure of three sections: a Song Box, Story Box and Sound Box. I was keen to bring in new writers, new voices, and new songs, rather than always using existing songs, which had been the practice with this series. Nancy was an obvious talent to call upon – she can write a song about anything: give her the theme and she can't help herself! She'll find the unexpected angle that hooks you immediately. What's more, she was a primary school teacher at the time, au fait with the *Hopscotch* audience and the curriculum.

Nancy wrote many programmes for this series. Her *Hopscotch* stories, poems and songs had her hallmark elegance, clarity and quirky humour.

Garden opens one eye, one eye, one eye,
Garden opens one eye, says, "I give you snowdrops".
> *Snowdrops, Snowdrops, peeping through the green,*
> *What a long, long winter it has been.*
>> *But Garden he grumbles, Oh, Winter is deep,*
>> *And he pulls the covers over him and goes back to sleep.*

Garden opens two eyes, two eyes, two eyes,
Garden opens two eyes, says, "I give you crocuses".
> *Crocuses, Crocuses, in purple and in gold,*
> *Wave so bravely in the morning cold.*
>> *But Garden he grumbles, Oh, Winter is deep,*
>> *And he pulls the covers over him and goes back to sleep.*

Garden shakes his shoulders, shoulders, shoulders,
Garden shakes his shoulders, says, "I give you daffodils".
> *Daffodils, Daffodils, dancing on the hill,*
> *Laughing, laughing, never feel the chill.*
>> *But Garden he grumbles, Oh, Winter is deep,*
>> *And he pulls the covers over him AND WE TICKLE HIS FEET.*

Anne Lorne Gillies was our excellent presenter, story-teller and singer. The BBC didn't have keyboards available – the work of the Education Department was increasingly low budget – so I used to borrow my brother's keyboard, which he would kindly deliver to the BBC Queen Street studio in Edinburgh, so that Anne could accompany herself, with bells, strings or even flutes, and sundry tinkling magical effects.

For the *Hopscotch* Story Box, Nancy created the character of a mouse who, like a child, was learning about the world and its wonders. As ever with her writing, the language was subtle and engaging, delighting its young audience. I remember a senior producer questioning the word *caput* in one of Nancy's scripts, written on the theme of time and clocks: in the story, a grandfather clock ceased to work. It was pointed out that a child wouldn't understand such a word. But Nancy grasped that we don't always have to know intellectually what language means in order to understand it – we can discover meaning instinctively. I kept caput in, and when I played the programme to my pre-school age son, he roared with laughter at the new word, understanding it from its context, revelling in its sound. For months afterwards, he used *caput* instead of broken, whenever he possibly could!

Nancy also wrote stories for other radio series I produced, including history based programmes, written as stories – one on The Maid of Norway, and another about the Jacobites, the latter taking Lady Nairn's beautiful song 'The White Rose of June' as the starting point. I visited Nancy's class at Bruntsfield Primary School, to observe her using these programmes with her pupils. She never raised her voice – simply clapped her hands to gain attention. She was completely in command within the comfortable, happy atmosphere she created for her pupils.

Sadly, Nancy no longer has all the copies of these scripts I commissioned, and the BBC hasn't kept them either. I still have cassette tapes of the programmes, but they are so old – a quarter of a century – that the sound has deteriorated, and is now very muffled. However, it may be possible to transcribe the material from these recordings before they finally fade forever. A beautiful book of children's stories and poems could be salvaged from them, complete with songs.

Some twenty years later, I was reading my poetry and singing my own songs at the Ullapool Book Festival. Nancy was there, at breakfast one morning in the legendary Ceilidh Place, and she had the whole dining room of writers in fits of laughter at her rendition of her brilliantly subversive, satirical song 'They Sent A Wumman'.

> *Ah sent for the doctor, Ah telephoned the day,*
> *The doctor wis an affa time a-comin,*
> *Ah sent for the doctor, but sorry for to say,*
> *A doctor never came – they sent a wumman.*
> > *But Ah let her, make me better,*
> > *Then Ah asked her could she no get intae nursing?*
> > *Ah sent for the doctor, but when she went away,*
> > *Ah couldnae understand why she wis cursin.*

A couple of years later, I called round to her flat in Edinburgh one day, in search of that song. I'm part of a trio, called Madge Wildfire, with Patsy Seddon and Kathy Stewart, and wanted to sing it to them, with a view to including it in our repertoire. Typically generous, Nancy sent me away with a whole sheaf of her songs, including the hilarious 'Brickie's Ballad', in praise of a brickie's bum! She sings it with all the joy of a woman revelling in her sexuality, going about her daily business, lusting after a male posterior cleavage.

> *It was early one May on a fine summer's day*
> *Gaun ma messages tae Willie Low's,*
> *I raised up ma eyes where the guys in the skies*
> *On the scaffolding stood an they posed.*
> > *I saw me a view of a bright rosy hue*
> > *Ah couldnae get oot ae ma mind,*
> > *When his shirt left his breeks and I saw the baith cheeks*
> > *O a braw barry brickie's behind.*

Nothing predatory or salacious here, simply downright earthy celebration.

In all of Nancy's writing her heart beats for humanity. She is steadfast in her commitment to giving voice to the underdog; in her blistering exposure of corrupt politicians; her deep concern for the environment; championing of her Caithness roots, Scotland's culture and its great diversity; all of which she achieves with consummate skill, and an irresistible desire to subvert and celebrate. She is a true Makar, yet, like so many of Scotland's great women, she is an unsung heroine, a treasure in our midst.

WHAT DID YOU SAY?

A Wee Primer on Caithness Language
A Peedie Bittie on Kaitness Spek

Nancy Nicolson

Some of you may come from Caithness and have no need of this advice. Others may ken different versions of Scots Language. If you have little experience of the Scots and Caithness speech, I do hope it will help you get a taste of our Northern tongue. Here I have called upon the teaching of John Ross of Wick High School, my English teacher in 1958.

There is a Glossary (p.209), a list of Caithness words used in the book plus, just for fun, a hundred favourites I had chosen working as a Scots Language Ambassador in Schools. SLAS is a function of Education Scotland.

Caithness and other forms of Scots Language do not, in general, employ apologetic apostrophes. If a letter is 'missing', it's not meant to be there.

Orthography: How can we write words in a way that adequately describes speech which exists purely in sound? The sound and the printed word are entirely different actualities. It's akin to singing a building or dancing a dictionary. But I'll have a go.

Pronunciation: The softening of J and G is a unique feature of Kaitness spek: 'Jim, John, Jane, George', become 'Chim, Chon, Chane, Cheorge'. A 'jar of jam' becomes a 'char o cham'.

Pronunciation of 'i': That's a big pig – Aat's a beeg peeg. 'Big, dig, fig, pig, pin' become 'beeg, deeg, feeg, peeg, peen'.

Pronunciation of 'o' or 'oa'; I am on the road home – A'm on e rod hom. 'Road, load, home, stone, bone' are pronounced 'rod, lod, hom, ston, bon'.

One Kaitness vowel sound is very hard to describe. In English it may be written 'ea', 'ay' or 'ae'. You need to hear it. It's a diphthong, moving from 'i' as in 'pin' to 'ee' as in 'been'. I like to write it as 'ey'.

'Hay, bay, eat, great' become 'hey, bey, eyt, greyt', and the Scots word 'fae' becomes 'fey'.

'Made, name, head, able, table, stable' become 'meyd, neyme, heyd, eyble, teyble, steyble'.

General differences: The first person singular 'I, I'm, I'll' become 'A, A'm, A'll' or 'Ah, Ah'm, Ah'll'.

The English common words 'the, this, that, there,' lose 'th' to become 'e, iss, aat or at, ere'. I and many others use 'e' for 'the'. George Gunn uses 'ay'. His version better reflects the actual vowel sound. Mine better reflects the unaccented throwaway lightness of the word. So here's me getting in a raivel already, and no wonder. I am trying to express language that is spoken and heard in a written form, to be read. Yes, we're dancing a dictionary.

At's hid! – That's it!

Kaitness, like its folk, can be contradictory. Here the language knocks 'th' off 'that', then changes 'it' to 'id' and adds an initial 'h' to make 'hid'. It's a lot easier to say than to explain.

Faar are ye goin and faa's gon wi ye? We substitute an 'f' sound for 'wh' in many words. 'Who, what, when, where?' become 'faa, fit, fan, faar'.

Diminutives: Caithness is rich in diminutives. In most cases these are as much endearments as descriptions of size. 'Peedie' meaning 'little' is found in Caithness and Orkney, with the variation 'peerie' in Shetland. It derives from the French 'petit'. Long ago, Westward-bound French seafarers faced the dangers of the Pentland Firth and Northern waters rather than sail the English Channel. They employed local sea-pilots who, after the voyage, took French words home with them. The suffixes -ag, or -agie show one or two degrees of smallness. Folk will refer to a boy as a 'peedie little wee boyagie' thus diminishing the 'boy' five times. Lassagie is the female form. George Gunn is wont to address me as 'Nancagee'.

Grammar: Grammatically, in Caithness we can say 'a alsatian', 'a artist', 'a aaful loud noise'.

There are also peculiarities in singular and plural words.

What would be in English a singular form of a verb is paired with a plural subject:

'Chefs have very sharp knives' – 'Chefs hes richt sharp knifes'. (hes – has)

'All those horses have iron shoes on their hooves.' – 'Aal aat horshes hes iron shoes on thur hoofs.'

'These cows are going to the show. The both of them are in the stock lorry.'

'Aat coos is goin til e show. E both o thum is in e stock larry.'

Many folk believe that grammar is outdated, just a field for the pernickety. Not so. We neglect grammar at our peril, not only in Scots but English too. Without it we may soon not be able to understand or be understood.

A simple piece of punctuation can make a sentence say exactly the opposite of what was intended. Granny Stewart illustrated this for me in a story when I was a bairn.

A teacher was scolding a boy who had made an error in punctuation. She told him he was lazy and stupid. She ordered him to punctuate a sentence. Aiming to humiliate him, she wrote on the blackboard: 'The teacher says the boy is a fool', and handed him the chalk. The boy thought for a moment and punctuated thus: 'The teacher', says the boy, 'is a fool.'

Yes, do take care of your grammar, in whatever language you operate.

Bexley Terrace, busy with bairns on a summer day in the 1890s
(© Johnston Collection)

BAIRNS

GRANDA SAID

Nancy Nicolson

INTRO.

VERSES

I used tae live in a far off place when I was just a lass-kie, The wind drew ros-es up-on ma face an the air was sweet wi whis——ky, But I did grow and I did go, my For-tune for to try, Doon the ir-on lane faar the Sooth bound train rolled off in-to the sky.——

Granda Said

I used tae live in a far off place when I was just a lasskie,
The wind drew roses upon ma face an the air was sweet wi whisky,
But I did grow and I did go, my fortune for to try.
Doon the iron lane faar the Sooth bound train rolled off into the sky.

Ma Granda said 'Now the place to go is Edinburgh City,
A've been there twice and ma advice is that's the place, ma pretty,
Hid's fine an beeg, it's capital, it's bonnier than Weeck',
Ma Granda's fill o good advice, an he's no short o cheek!

Ma Granda said 'See the fine tram cars', but I could not keep that pledge,
 Aal I saa wis a beeg red bus that slipped along lek a sledge.
An I did grow and I did go, pursue the modern course,
But milk and beer and polis here are cairted by a horse.

'There's a clock all made oot o flooers', he said, so go and see it Nansie
When did A get there? A'll tell ye, two violets past a pansy.
An I did grow and I did go an view fair Princes Street,
But cultivated thistles wid made crofter Granda greet.

'Take a trip to the Zoo'. ma granda said, 'See the wondrous works o God',
But the highway roared wi the works of Ford, and I never got ower that rod,
But I did grow and I did go and see that wondrous pleyce,
 Faar tigers, bears an elephants, are gey amazing beyce.

'Watch oot for two-legged rats', said he , but A can an A must declare, Toon
folk are nice tho they live lek mice in warrens they caal a stair.
An I did grow and I did go, the citizens to see,
I keen did stare at people there but nobody looked at me.

Thank you Granda. This was the first song I ever wrote, for the Edinburgh Folk Club Song-writing competition in 1976. Sheila Douglas's brilliant 'O Mither Mither' was the worthy winner. I liked that song so much it appears on my CD *Rhyme and Reason*. I took for my subject the teasing advice that my Granda gave me for my first trip to Edinburgh when I was six.

THE STUSHIE — Nancy Nicolson

INTRO.

VERSES

1. The close wis teemin wi the bair-ens far the stair, There wis keepie up-pie, collie-buckie, ropes and peev-er there, They wer singin, bawl-in, fechtin, crawlin, could nae see the flair, And they cried a bar-ley.

2. An Ku-mar got a Pizza, Ky-lie got a pie, Jock got a cha-pat-ti an a big stir-fry, Su-Wong got a hag-gis sup-per, double chips for-bye, An they aa breenged in.

The Stushie

The close wis teemin wi the bairens fae the stair,
There wis keepie-uppie, colliebuckie, ropes and peever there,
They were singin, bawlin, fechtin, crawlin, couldnae see the flair,
And they cried a barley.

An Kumar got a Pizza, Kylie got a pie,
Jock got a chapatti an a big stir-fry,
Su-Wong got a haggis supper, double chips forbye,
An they aa breenged in.

An the pizza it wis mega, an the pie wis braw,
The chapatti it wis barry an the stir-fry braw an aa,
But the haggis it wis bowfin an the chips were mingin too,
Whaur's the cludgie?

They were wabbit they were peelie-wallie, greetin, bokin too,
A wheen o glaikit eejits wi een bigger than their mou,
An I warrant they'll go mental when they catch wee Su,
Whit a stushie!

The song was written in early 1990s for a BBC schools programme on Scots language. The remit was to write a song about Scots language not in the past but today. And not in the country but in a city. It had to include food and games. One element I loved while teaching in Edinburgh was the variety of nations and cultures my bairns came from.

The words bairn, film, girl and others, can be pronounced as we usually do in standard English. However in many forms of Scots language an extra little sound comes in to give an extra syllable as in bairen, filem, girel. (Maybe you think it sounds more like bairin, filim, giril.) If you want to impress folk, just tell them the wee sound is a schwa, part of phonetics, the science of sound in speech. That wee 'e' letter and sound is a schwa, a neutral vowel in an unaccented syllable.

LISTEN TAE THE TEACHER

Nancy Nicolson

REFRAIN

Listen tae the teach-er, din-na say dinna, Listen tae the teach-er, din-na say hoose

Listen tae the teach-er, ye can-na say manna, Listen tae the teacher, ye maunna say moose.

VERSES

He's five-year-auld, he's aff tae school, Fairm-er's bairn wi a pen-cil an a rule, His teach-er scoffs when he says 'hoose', The word is 'house' you sil-ly little goose.

He tells his ma when he gets back, He saa a 'mouse' in an auld cairt-track. Faith-er lauchs fae the stack-yaird dyke, Yon's a moose, ye daft wee tyke.

Listen Tae The Teacher

CHORUS
Listen tae the teacher, dinna say dinna,
Listen tae the teacher, dinna say hoose,
Listen tae the teacher, ye canna say maunna,
Listen tae the teacher, ye maunna say moose.

He's five-year-auld, he's aff tae school,
Fairmer's bairn wi a pencil an a rule,
His teacher scoffs when he says 'hoose',
The word is 'house' you silly little goose.
    He tells his ma when he gets back
    He saa a 'mouse' in an auld cairt-track,
    His faither lauchs fae the stack-yaird dyke,
    Yon's a moose, ye daft wee tyke.

Listen tae the Teacher ...

He bit his lip an shut his mooth,
Which wan could he trust for truth?
He took his burden ower the hill
Tae auld grey Geordie o the mill.
    An did they mock thee for thy tongue,
    Wi them sae auld an thoo sae young?
    They werena makkin a fuil o thee,
    Makkin a fuil o themsels ye see.

Listen tae the Teacher ...

This song is first and foremost for the teacher who glowered at me when I said 'Hoose' in class in 1948. I was so ashamed of myself that I didn't answer a question for two weeks! I wrote the song in mid-1970s. Yes, I am slow to anger. In the song I make it a boy, and write in Lowland Scots, as that was the language of the first audience that would hear it. I entered it for a song-writing competition for the *Edinburgh Evening News*. To my surprise and great delight, it won. More important than the shield I won that night was the enduring friendship of the two runners-up, Andy Mitchell and Denis Alexander. The song is now included in the official curricular resources for Scottish Teachers, 'The Kist'. Such a sweet result! Recorded on *Rhyme and Reason*, 1990 .

Say *hoose* tae the faither, *house* tae the teacher,
Moose tae the fairmer, *mouse* tae the preacher,
Where ye're young it's weel for you
Tae dae in Rome as Romans do.
      But when ye growe an ye are auld
      Ye needna dae as ye are tauld,
      Nor trim yer tongue tae suit yon dame
      Scorns the language o her hame.

    Listen tae the Teacher ...

Then teacher thought that he wis fine,
He kept in step he stayed in line,
An faither said that he wis gran,
Spoke his ain tongue like a man.
      An when he grew an made his choice,
      He chose his Scots, his native Voice,
      An I charge ye tae dae likewise,
      Spurn yon puir misguided cries.

    Listen tae the Teacher...

Nancy's first school, School Class Group, Old South School, Wick
(© Johnston Collection)

TEACHER LOVES ME   Nancy Nicolson

INTRO.

La la la lala la la la.

VERSE 1

Teach-er loves me, this I know, eve-ry day she tells me so;

In my jot-ter, my dear Miss marks each sum with a big red kiss.

Yes, Teach-er loves me,—— Yes, Teach-er loves me,——

Yes, Teach-er loves me, her kiss-es tell me so——

VERSE 2

Teach-er needs me, I can tell, Since the day the Heid-ie fell, I

tripped him up, he went hi length, Teach-er said 'Oh, give me strength!'

Yes, Teach-er needs me,—— yes, Teach-er needs me——

Yes, Teach-er needs me, she says I give her strength.——

Teacher Loves Me

melody: Jesus loves me

Teacher loves me, this I know,
every day she tells me so,
In my jotter my dear Miss
marks each sum with a big red kiss.

Yes, Teacher loves me, yes, Teacher loves me,
Yes Teacher loves me, her kisses tell me so.

Teacher needs me, I can tell,
Since the day the Heidie fell,
I tripped him up, he went his length,
Teacher said, 'Oh give me strength!'

Yes, Teacher needs me, yes Teacher needs me
Yes, Teacher needs me, she says I give her strength.

I know Teacher likes me best,
So much better than the rest,
She can't get enough of me,
Keeps me in til half past three.

Yes, Teacher likes me, yes, Teacher likes me
Yes, Teacher likes me, keeps me til half past three

She adores me, and why not?
Look at all the charm I've got!
I brought her a fine fat frog,
She looked up, said 'Oh my God!'

These are the pupils I remember with great fondness, and always a smile. There were so many brilliant bairns with personality, charm, brains, and humour. They proved daily that Education as we are charged to deliver it in schools, was not and is not fit for purpose. Teaching P1, P2 & P3 in Midlothian and Edinburgh with too many to list, but today I think with fond memories of bairns in Midlothian, in Edinburgh, and the first of the genre, in my very first teaching post, in Granton.

Teacher adores me, Teacher adores me,
Teacher adores me, that's why she calls me God.

(OCCASIONALLY you may want to repeat first verse)

Teacher loves me, this I know,
every day she tells me so
In my jotter my dear Miss
marks each sum with a big red kiss.

$$2 + 2 = 5 X$$

BAIRN BROON, MAW BROON   Nancy Nicolson

INTRO.

VERSES

1

Bairn Broon, Maw Broon, boss-es o the hoose Keep the rest in order when they're on the loose,

Glebe Street's joy, Glebe Street's pride, Twaa strong wee-min side by side.

Maw has the pow-er, Bairn has the spark, Hour by hour—, dawn til dark,

Bairn sees the Fu-ture, Maw kens the past, They laugh lang-est, they laugh last.

2

Bairn Broon, Maw Broon, boss-es o the hoose Keep the rest in order when they're on the loose

Gran-paw's smokin in his eas-y chair, Splashin ash aa ower the flair

Maw gies him pelters for the aw-fy stoor, 'You sit there juist fil-in aa ma floor.'

Bairn says 'Smelly, smokin like a lum.' Granpaw steeks his pipe oot, he's un-der Bairn's thumb.

Bairn Broon, Maw Broon

To traditional melody 'Castles in the Air'

Bairn Broon, Maw Broon, bosses o the hoose
 Keep the rest in order when they're on the loose,
Glebe Street's joy, Glebe Street's pride,
Twae strong weemin side by side
 Maw has the power, Bairn has the spark,
 Hour by hour, dawn til dark,
 Bairn sees the future, Maw kens the past,
 They laugh langest, they laugh last

Bairn Broon, Maw Broon, bosses o the hoose Keep the rest in
order when they're on the loose,
Granpaw's smokin in his easy chair,
Splashin ash aa ower the flair,
 Maw gies- him -pelters for the awfy stoor,
 'You sit there,
 filin aa ma floor.' (*floor to rhyme with stoor*)
 Bairn says 'Smelly, smokin like a lum',
 Granpaw-steeks his-pipe-oot -,
 he's-under Bair-n 's thumb

Bairn Broon, Maw Broon, bosses o the hoose
Keep the rest in order when they're on the loose,
Maggie bocht some braw new shoes,
Got them for a bargain , cannae lose.
 Maw says 'Maggie, Oh, they're awfy high'
 'But ma new lad's a real tall guy',
 Bairn says 'Maggie, aye , they're smert,
 But tak- the- half- price- label -aff afore ye stert' .

In many years of reading 'The Broons' I noticed that a problem might be identified by Maw or one of the adults, but it would be Bairn who solved it. The song was written before 2014 when Nicola Sturgeonbecame First Minister. Before that FM Alex Salmond , was considered the more daunting debater.

Bairn Broon, Maw Broon, bosses o the hoose
Keep the rest in order when they're on the loose,
Paw thocht up a braw new scheme,
Growin- rasps- an- makin- jam, Whit a dream
       Maw says, 'Paw, the birds'll eat them aa,'
       Paw says, 'The twins'll scare the birds awa'
       Bairn says, *'Ye'd be* better wi a craw,
       Twins'll eat them raw by raw'

Bairn Broon, Maw Broon, bosses o the hoose,
Keep the rest in order when they're on the loose,
I ask ye, now, widnae it be good ,
Wi Bair-en Broon and Maw Broon tae rule in Holyrood?
       First Minister's Questions wid be a better deal,
       Trust the Broons tae keep it real,
       Trust the Broons tae keep them aa in check,
       Maw can tak on Nicola an Bairn taks Eck!

repeat last 4 lines

A WISH FOR THE WORLD   Nancy Nicolson

INTRO.

VERSE 1

I have a good and pleas-ant life In all the hills and toons o Fife, But
when I see poor peop-le's strife I weep for all the world.——

REFRAIN

Al — le — lu — ja, Al — le — lu — ja,
Al — le — lu — ja, Al-le — lu — ja ——

VERSE 2

I wish them wat-er in a cup, And all their riv-ers be filled up, I
wish them wat-er in a cup And thirst-y nev-er more.——

A Wish for the World

To the air of the Gaelic song, 'The Christ Child's Lullaby'

I have a good and pleasant life
In all the hills and toons o Fife,
But when I see poor people's strife
I weep for all the world.

Alleluja, Alleluja, Alleluja, Alleluja,

I wish them water in a cup,
And all their rivers be filled up
I wish them water in a cup
And thirsty never more

Alleluja, ...

I wish all people had a home,
Cosy roof and walls of stone,
I wish all people had a home
And never more to roam

Alleluja, ...

I wish the World the chance to learn,
To read and write and grow and earn,
I wish the World the chance to learn,
And make themselves a life

Alleluja, ...

Written 1999 or 2000, along with the bairns of Headwell Special School in Dunfermline, Fife. I was working in Fife with The New Makars Trust, Director Gifford Lind, and had been sent to Headwell School for children with Special Needs. It was nearing Christmas. I asked the bairns what would be their Christmas wish if they had all the money and all the power in the world. Would they wish for all the toys advertised on TV? These bairns had many challenges, some physically handicapped, some with learning difficulties. Would they wish for new legs so they didn't need a wheelchair, or hands that could hold a pencil properly? They got on to a higher plane of thought than I could ever have guessed at! I was nearly in tears of wonder and humility by the end of the session.

DEAR CUMMIE — Nancy Nicolson

INTRO

VERSES

My thanks for the tie—, so spot-less and bright; The shirt is im-mac-u-late,

gleam-ing and white, With ne-ver a speck on the black vel-vet suit, But

when, Cum-mie, where are my fin-est dress boots?

REFRAIN

O Cum-mie, Dear Cum-mie, now how could you so Out to fine com-pan-y

send me to go, That had to be trig from my head to my toe, In

rock-scored and lum-bering, thun-der-ing, blun-der-ing, Nav-vy's salt-wat-er-stained

rack-et-y boots?

Dear Cummie

My thanks for the tie, so spotless and bright,

The shirt is immaculate, gleaming and white ,

With never a speck on the black velvet suit,

But where, Cummie, where are my finest dress boots?

CHORUS

> *O Cummie, Dear Cummie, now how could you so*
>
> *Out to fine company send me to go,*
>
> *That had to be trig from my head to my toe,*
>
> *In rock-scored and lumbering, thundering, blundering,*
>
> *Navvy's salt-water-stained tackety boots?*

This town that makes such a career of dismay,

That all it contains is so barren and grey,

That when it's not hidden by biting salt spray

Is hammered by gales they call "breezes".

> *O Cummie ...*

In all the weeks spent in this grim town's confinement

Was Sarah, the only sweet note of refinement,

The one ray of sunshine to lighten my day,

Now I'm bidden to dine up Breadalbane's fine Brae.

I wrote the song after reading an article by editor Alan Hendry in *The John O'Groat Journal* on the 150th anniversary in 2000 of Robert Louis Stevenson's birth Nov 13, 1850:

Thomas Stevenson the marine engineer and his 17-year old son Robert Louis were working in Wick. They were invited to dine with Sheriff Russell at Breadalbane Terrace. The Sheriff's daughter Sarah, 16, was intelligent and beautiful. According to a letter to his mother Robert had taken a wee shine to her. Robert, very fussy about his clothes, wrote to his former nurse Cummie (Alison Cunningham) to send his dress clothes from Edinburgh. She sent everything ... except his dress boots! Robert Louis liked to look trig. He cared as much for the right footwear as any young man. He wrote Cummie a very stern letter, scolding her for her 'treachery'! I have made his letter into this song. We have it on good authority that RL pronounced his name 'Lewis'... as did Louis Armstrong.

O Cummie ...

I step on the flagstones and shrink at the racket
Of coarse bullock-hide and of clattering tackets,
The gulls of Breadalbane are mocking my stride
And rolls of wild laughter resound from the Tide.

O Cummie ...

There's me, and the Devil, betrayed by our feet,
I'm wanting my fine boots so smooth and so neat
Oh, Sarah, Sweet Sarah, don't look down I pray
For my feet are in boots that are clarted in clay.

O Cummie...

HISTORY & PLACES

CASTLE OF SPITE

The Story of Carbisdale Castle.

A Duke an improver, a far north estate, and greed beyond avarice dreams,
The white sheep and misery, murder and hate, and blood that ran in streams,
That was the Sutherlands, Dukes o Dunrobin, who tortured beyond all forbearance,
and left like a scar on their line & their blood, the terrible ghost of the Clearance.

Mary Caroline, widow of Baird, knew just how to land on her feet,
Knew how to gather possessions and power, to keep them intact & complete,
She's wedded the widower Duke, what a catch, and off to the North she did race,
But there she discovered his next generation could not stand the sight of her face.

The Duke he was poorly, the Duke up'd & died, & left all he owned to his wife
The family railed at such a divide, and rose up in contest and strife.
'We've been his fam-i-ly full thirty years, you are a lady-come-late,
We challenge your claim, we spit on your name, & trust to the lawyers your fate'.

The contest was cruel, the barbs they were harsh, dire deeds were done on each side,
For burning of documents not to her taste, she in Holloway brief did reside.
She loudly did claim that she must have a castle, befitting her station so grand,
And so it was granted, but must not be built in the County of fair Sutherland.

She hatch-ed her plot & each tittle & jot was planned & designed &created.
And high, O so high, on a on Rosshire hillside Sweet Carb–is-dale was situated
From ev–er-y track to Dunrobin and back, Carbisdale could not be missed,
And Carbisdale Castle in all of its glory, by sunlight & moonlight was kissed.

The Story of Carbisdale Castle: Mary Caroline Baird, Widow of the Duke of Sutherland, fell out with the Duke's Family at Dunrobin Castle. They insisted she must leave Dunrobin. At that she demanded that she have her own castle. The Sutherlands were vain about Dunrobin, so beautiful with its 365 windows. Mary Caroline bested them, and Carbisdale has 366 windows.
 The building bagan in 1906. Lady Mary built a square clock-tower with a clock on three of its four faces. The side facing Dunrobin had no clock... She would not 'give them the Time of Day'. With thanks to friends Ann and Robert Cross who told me about the change of border on a visit in 2012.

The stone was more golden, the form full of charm, & then as a sparkling crown,
The windows, one more than Dunrobin itself, would twinkle & gloat & look down.
The clocktow-er fair is ever so rare, a dial on three of four faces,
The wall to the North it is blank it is blind, surveying the Sutherlands' places.

'I won't give you comfort, I won't give you joy, I won't give you pleasure to pay,
Won't give you a button to use for a toy, won't give you a penny to play,
Won't give you a minute won't give you an hour, won't give you a second I say,
Won' t give you a moment won't give you a tick, won't give you the time of the day'.

Now, she was no hero, a spitful of spite, of greed and of avarice made,
But strength to her arm, she caused pain & alarm to the Sutherlands & their brigade
Who burnt from their houses such fine Highland folk, evicted & banished them thence
To furnish the hills with the flocks of white sheep, for pounds & for shillings & pence

In all of this ploy the greatest of joy, revenge serv-ed cold as a chill,
For now civil servants just add to the foy - they change county borders at will.
They shifted a border to give better order, So people, let me raise a dram,
For Carbisdale It is in SUTHERLAND now, So thanks, Mary Caroline, Ma'am.

repeat last 2 lines.

WEECK AN POLTNEY   Nancy Nicolson

INTRO.

REFRAIN

Weeck an Polt-ney, Polt-ney an Weeck, Cheek by jowl an jowl by cheek, Weeck an Polt-ney, Polt-ney an Weeck, They Fished e Sil-ver Dar-lins,

VERSES

E Vi-kings sailed e North-ern Main, E Vi-kings, they gave Weeck ids name E Vi-kings kent e Fish-ing game, They Fished e Sil-ver Dar-lins

Weeck An Poltney

E Vikings sailed e Northern Main,
E Vikings, they gave Weeck ids name,
E Vikings kent e fishing game,
They fished e Silver Darlins

CHORUS
> Weeck an Poltney, Poltney an Weeck,
> Cheek by jowl an jowl by cheek,
> Weeck an Poltney, Poltney an Weeck,
> They fished e Silver Darlins.

A Skipper fey Serclad, crew fey Weeck,
A cook fey Keiss til bile yur beef,
Skipper fey Serclad, crew fey Weeck,
They fished e Silver Darlins.

> Weeck an Poltney ...

Darena go if ye meet a minister,
Evrychiel kens a minister's sinister,
Darena go if ye meet a minister
Til e Silver Darlins.

> Weeck an Poltney ...

E herrin rise up through e Blue
A hefty shot, a happy crew,

I was pleased to be asked in 2007 to sing for the Wick Harbour Festival. I could not find a Caithness song about the fishing, so made this one. Wick River divides the town in two, Wick to the North, Pulteneytown to the Sooth. The Herring fishing was a signal part of the Town's history. At one time Wick was the biggest herring port in the world, with over a thousand boats in the harbour. You could walk across the harbour from one side to the other on the decks of herring boats. My maternal Granda, Sanny Stewart fey Sarclet, then Hempriggs, sailed on *The Drift Fisher* the first steam drifter at sailed oot o Weeck. Ither Granda, Wullie Nicolson, was a carter taking barrels of herring up the long Shore Road.

A drammie in e Mountain Dew,
Til toast e Silver Darlins.

Weeck an Poltney ...

E Guttin Lassies knifes wid flash,
They packed e barrels wi silver stash,
Guttin Lassies knifes wid flash,
They packed e Silver Darlins.

Weeck an Poltney...

Id's saalty bleed at plays ids pert,
An saalty sweyt at makes ye smert,
An saalty tears at breaks yer hert
At peys for Silver Darlins.

Weeck an Poltney ...

Pulteneytown Harbour 1863 (© Johnston Collection)

HARD-BOILED EGGS   Nancy Nicolson

REFRAIN

"Hard-boiled eggs" says the hard-boiled wo-man ————— "hard cheese!"

"Hard-boiled eggs" says the hard-boiled wo-man ————— "hard cheese!"

"Hard-boiled eggs" says the hard-boiled wo-man. Sal-mon-el-la hurts the humans.

Can it tooch the ir-on wo-man ————— Hard cheese!

VERSES

You dip your sol-diers in the soft yolk. One's a gal and one's a

fel-la. Dip your sol-diers in the soft yolk

Call them Sam-an-El-la —————

Hard-Boiled Eggs

'Hard-boiled eggs' says the hard-boiled woman – 'hard cheese!'
'Hard-boiled eggs' says the hard-boiled woman – 'hard cheese!'
'Hard-boiled eggs' says the hard-boiled woman –
Salmonella harms the humans,
Can it touch the Iron Woman? – Hard Cheese!
> I dip my soldiers in the soft yolk,
> One's a gal and one's a fella.
> Dip my soldiers in the soft yolk,
> Call them Sam and Ella.

'Hard-boiled eggs' says the hard-boiled woman – 'hard cheese!' etc...
Listeria harms the humans,
Can it touch the Iron Woman? – Hard Cheese!
> I love my Brie, I love my blue-veined,
> Don't fear no Listeria,
> The thing that's makin me feel sick is
> Ministerial hysteria.

'Hard-boiled eggs' says the hard-boiled woman – 'hard cheese!' etc...
PSD, it harms the humans,
Can it touch the Iron Woman? – Hard Cheese!
> Was just about to eat an oyster,
> The oyster thus besought me
> If you think I am paralytic
> You should have seen the boy that caught me.

This song refers to food panics in the late 1980s. I wrote the song at that time. In the late 1980s, the era of Prime Minister Margaret Thatcher and Food minister Edwina Currie, there were outbreaks of different food poisonings, first Salmonella, then Listeria. There was also mention of PSD, Paralytic Shellfish Disease, and BSE, *Bovine Spongiform Encephalopathy*. Some politicians overstated the dangers, but PM Thatcher and Food Minister Currie insisted there was no great risk as long as we hard- boiled our eggs and stopped eating soft cheese! I can't remember what we thought their real agenda was, can you? Recorded on Rhyme and Reason, 1990

'Hard-boiled eggs' says the hard-boiled woman – 'hard cheese!' etc...
BSE, it harms the humans,
Can it touch the Iron Woman? – Hard Cheese!
       I sink my teeth intae a beefsteak,
       Scotch is best, ye ken,
       Just wan mad coo we've tae contend wi,
       An she lives at Number 10

'Hard-boiled eggs' says the hard-boiled woman – 'hard cheese!' etc...
Those germs just harm the humans .. etc
Can they touch the Iron Woman? –   Hard Cheese!
       It's not the folk who make the food
       that cause it to taste funny
       The filthy fingers in the mixture
       Are on the hands that JUST make money.

'Hard-boiled eggs' says the hard-boiled woman – 'hard cheese!' etc...
Those germs just harm the humans,
Can they touch the Iron Woman? Hard bloody cheese !!!

Peggy Sue (© Johnston Collection)

THE MIDNIGHT COVE

Nancy Nicolson

1. Out a-blow the Brae-head, far be-yond the quay, A roar-ing chasm in a cliff chis-eled by the sea, Warmed wi hu-man kind-ness, wel-comed wi a yarn, Wi Geor-die an wi Peg-gie an a dram-mie

2. Heart-ened by the whis-ky, Geor-die, like a bear, Growled his loud ap-pro-val That I had en-tered there, Pressed in-to my fro-zen hand a gill-ful in a tin, A bran-dy served in crys-tal was no sweet-er.

The Midnight Cove

Out below the Braehead, far beyond the quay,
A roaring chasm in a cliff, chiseled by the sea,
Warmed wi human kindness, welcomed wi a yarn
Wi Geordie and wi Peggy and a drammie.   .

Heartened by the whisky, Geordie, like a bear,
Growled his loud approval that I had ventured there,
Pressed into my frozen hand a gill-full in a tin,
A brandy served in crystal was no sweeter.

Tales and wild carousing, faces warmed by fire,
Sea forever roaring at the door that was not there,
Geordie told of poaching, Peggy sang of sprees,
A soiree in a palace was no finer.

Peggy danced a hornpipe from a matelot
Rescued from a sinking ship forty years ago,
Geordie cheered a wild "Hurrah", slapped my back with glee,
No Lord all in a castle could been prouder.

I tried a yarn of smugglers – "Ay, man, that's the way",
Peggy puffed her owld clay pipe, and still my tale held sway.
She said, "Ye hev the *coinneach*, man, ye hev the knack,
Ye'll tell anither tale anither morrow."

The Moon on her horizon lit that rocky hall,
Til past the hour of midnight oft I made that call,
We sailed the seas in story, high adventures won,
And Leaving Peg a sixpence to buy whisky.

Another song I wrote after reading that article in *The John o Groat Journal* on the 150th anniversary in 2000 of Robert Louis Stevenson's birth Nov 13, 1850. Marine engineer Thomas Stevenson was in Wick to build a breakwater in the bay. His son Robert Louis Stevenson was there as a trainee engineer.

  He fell in with a MacPhee family who lived in a cove on the Bay. He would buy a bottle of whisky for a sixpence, and spent many a sociable time with Geordie and Peggy Sue. There is a photo of the family in the cove in Wick Heritage Centre.

THE HEILAN HORSE — Nancy Nicolson

INTRO.

La la la la La la la la La la la la La la

VERSES

Wull-ie was an aa-ful man for show-in up the ney-bours,

Ay must hav the best o gear til help him wi his ley-bours, The

Fin-est beyce, the posh-est playce, or else his wife wid ant-le, She'd

no be seen wi less than best as long as Wull hed cend-le.

CHORUS

Must hev a hor-si-gie, strong-er an swack-er

Hand-som-er and her-ti-er and bon-ni-er an black-er. He

The Heilan Horse

Wullie was an aaful man for showin up e neybours,
Hed til hev e best o gear til help him wi his leybours,
The finest beyce, the poshest pleyce, or else his wife wid antle.
She'd no be seen wi less than best as long as Wull hed candle.
Must hev a horsigie, stronger an swacker,
Handsomer and hertier and bonnier an blacker.

He heerd there was a splendid meyre at Inverness's Horse Fair,
He took his gig an pocket book an swift he made his course there,
He met the man fae Wester Ross, he saw the pownie's peyces,
Indeed she was a paragon o all the horsey greyces.

She was a horsigie...

He perted wi his fifty pound but didna look so braa-lek,
When Wester-Ross says 'by the way. She only hass the Gaelic.
She will not answer to a word in English that is spoken
Tho perfect in all else detail, she iss not Language-broken.

She was a horsigie...

When Wull said 'Hup, the ither shalties turned their heyds to Larboard,'
Heilan shook her shiny mane and cantered off to Starboard.

Recorded on *Rhyme and Reason*, 1990. Granny Stewart told the story of her brother Peter Forbes, a young ploughman on a big farm in Easter Ross in the first decade of the 20th century. In those days farmers showed off about their horses as they might today about their cars, and had to have the best! The Boss came home from the horse sale with a reputedly fabulous horse... but once yoked in the plough she would not perform.

The first ploughman, the second, and the third all tried, but she seemed determined to frustrate them. Then Peter asked the Boss if he could try. Boss and senior ploughmen all laughed and disparaged his chances, the 'loon', the youngest, the least experienced of them all. What could he do? 'Off you go, then', said the boss, as they all watched, waiting for him to make a fool of himself. Peter approached the horse, petted her, rubbed her nose and whispered in her ear. Off she went as nice as nine-pence and Peter ploughed a perfect furrow! He had talked to the horse and spoken her instructions in Gaelic!

Haud oot said Wull, but she held in, The ploo it hit a rock then,
Brankin new, Ah'm tellin you, the fancy ploo it broke then.

All for the horsigie...

She broke the Back Delivery that Wullie set sich store by,
She cowped the bogie in the burn, The maistress wi it foreby.
Bert the post was on the brig, an Bertie he was lookin.
By 6 o clock the county kent Hersel hed got a drookin

All for the horsigie...

Ye micht heve thocht the Heilan Horsie wid be in disgreyce no, Ye micht
hev thocht that Wullie wid be feyred to show his feyce now.
Wull, he smiles and claps the meyre, 'Ah live in perfect peyce now.
The horsie wis the only wan pit Maggie in her pleyce now!

All for the horsigie.

Horse Drawn Plough (© Johnston Collection)

THE BERRYIN AT BLAIR Nancy Nicolson

INTRO

REFRAIN

A'm at the berry-in, the berry-in at Blair, There's
berr-ies in ma pooch-es an there's berr-ies in ma hair, Sae
whit dae ye think I look like? Well, just think, Ma
Fing-ers an ma pooch-es an ma hair's aa pink.

VERSE

Whit's my busi-ness? Just you ask it,
A've tae pit the berr-ies in the bask-et,
Din-na tak the wiz-ened yins, din-na tak the green; Just
tak the bon-nie rid yins in a-tween.

The Berryin at Blair

A'm at the berryin, the berryin at Blair,
There's berries in ma pooches an there's be berries in ma hair,
Sae whit dae ye think I look like? Well just think,
Ma fingers an ma pooches an ma hair's aa pink.

Whit's my business? Just you ask it,
A've tae pit the berries in the basket,
Dinnae tak the wizened yins , dinnae tak the green,
Just tak the bonnie rid yins in atween.

A'm at the berryin, the berryin at Blair,
There's berries in ma pooches an there's be berries in ma hair,
Sae whit dae ye think I look like? Well just think,
Ma fingers an ma pooches an ma hair's aa pink!

Written for Radio Scotland Schools Programme *Hopscotch*, producer Gerda Stevenson, in early 1990s.

Maggie's Pit Ponies

They stand with the miners, the Hunterson picket,
Steady and staunch and unbroken,
Til through the dark morning, a clatter of hooves,
And Thatcher's most treacherous Token,
The swing of a baton, the Chief 's curt command,
The wall of horseflesh did not falter
A mountain of muscle at seventeen hands,
by the Spur and the Bit and the Halter

CHORUS
Here come the cavalry, here come the troops,
Here come Maggie's Pit Ponies,
Watch for the batons, boys, watch for the boots,
An watch yer back, Miner Johnnie.

This horse is not wicked, this horse is not wild,
Trained to obedience and order,
Walks soft as a lamb past a wee little child,
So why would he trample my Brother?
He's trained to obedience, the spur and the bit,
Answers the heel and the hand,
And they in their chance, they will march, run and dance.
To the auld iron wumman's command.

Here come the Cavalry…

While teaching in Midlothian throughout the Miners' Strike of 1984-5, I was President of Midlothian EIS (Educational Institute of Scotland, the Teachers' Union). After an EIS meeting in Edinburgh, some EIS Rank and File, a left-wing grouping, were watching TV footage of police horses charging the picket lines at Hunterston Power Station. City pals said, 'Look at those bloody horses'. I, fae a croft that had working Clydesdales, retorted, 'There's nothing bloody about the horses. They are just doing what they've been trained to do.' Then I realised that applied just as much to the laddies on their backs. I told my man Denness when I got home. He said 'Ay, Some bloody Pit Ponies!' Denness was the son of a Leith Docker, strong in the Dockers' Union.

This man is not wicked this man is not mean,
Puts on a chequerband cap. He joined to serve,
Justice and God and the Queen,
And to feed the two bairns in his lap.
But he's trained to obedience, Yes sir and yes ma'am.
Boys in blue, they're uniformed forces.
Must jump to the bidding of Steely Madame.
On the same bloody rein as the horses.

Here come the cavalry...

In muddy welsh dawn, cold Midlothian morning,
Bitter dark Yorkshire day-breaking,
See brother face brother and father face son
In conflict was none of their making.
For Mac lit the fuse on the charge Maggie planned,
The chasm divided a nation.
Now she prostitutes law just to strengthen her hand
And Justice is dead out of fashion.

Here come the cavalry...

193 OILMEN FEARED DEAD

5 a.m.

Piper Alpha platform blown apart

By DAVID STEELE and IAIN LUNDY

Act fast, Newton demands

Travel firm fail

Sobbing woman greets survivor

By DAVID STEELE

FR. Lt. HODGSON

RIG BLAST LATEST

SAFE — a wife hugs her oilman husband after he was flown into Aberdeen with other survivors from the platform blast.

ANOTHER PICTURE — PAGE 12

Serious accidents part of life on rigs

THE Piper Alpha oil production platform.

Piper Alpha Disaster 1988 (*Press and Journal*)

WHO PAYS THE PIPER? Nancy Nicolson

REFRAIN

Who pays the Pip-er, who pays the Pip-er
Who pays the Pip-er, who calls the tune?
Who pays the Pip-er, what is the fee?
Flames on the wat-er, death on the sea—

VERSES

And the tune is old and has al-ways told How the
great, brave and bold they do flour-ish— How
brave-ly they gam-ble with oth-er men's lives, And
pro-fit as oth-er men per-ish.—

Who Pays the Piper?

CHORUS

Who Pays the Piper, who Pays the Piper,
Who Pays the Piper, who calls the tune?
Who Pays the Piper, what is the fee?
Flames on the water, death on the sea.

And the tune is old and has always told
How the great, brave and bold they do flourish,
How bravely they gamble with other men's lives
And profit as other men perish.

Who Pays the Piper...

And the tune resounds and is always found
Where the ground receives yet another
Father of dazed and despairing young bairns,
Or son of a desolate mother.

Who Pays the Piper....

And the price is dear for the folk who fear,
And who bear the burden of sorrow,
For those who are lost where the graph of the cost
Meets the graph of rich pickings tomorrow.

Who Pays the Piper...

I wrote 'Who Pays the Piper' following the Piper Alpha disaster in 1988 where 167 men lost their lives. I suggest you read George Gunn's poem 'For the 167 Dead of Piper Alpha'. George has worked on Oil Rigs, not as a visiting artist, but to earn a wage. His eye is clear. He paints a searing picture. 'Who Pays the Piper' forms part of the 'Piper Alpha Memorial Exhibition in Aberdeen'. Recorded on *Rhyme and Reason*, 1990.

DON'T CALL MAGGIE — Nancy Nicolson

Don't call Maggie a Cat It's dreadful of you to say that, For
Cats are soft and Cats are warm, Ne-ver did you an-y harm, And
it would cause the cats al-arm If you called Maggie a Cat.

This was written mid-1980s. Following a revolt among a number of former friends in Cabinet, Margaret Thatcher stood down as Prime Minister on November 28, 1990. She was missed by some, but not by others.One surprising set of people who in one sense regretted her leaving, were the songwriters of Britain... we'd lost our best target! Spring 2013, Ritz Hotel, London, an old woman died. Margaret Thatcher in her time had ruined many lives. Those at the sharp end can be forgiven for finding not just solace, but a lesson, in the song.

She has been branded 'Cat; cow; snake; bitch'. You may know more. I went to teach in a new school in 1988.

 The headmaster asked me to sing the song at Assembly one morning. Why? I believe it was to demonstrate that the word Bitch has a literal meaning and is not necessarily a swear word. The Heidie, a stalwart of the EIS, teachers' union, was not keen on Thatcher or what she stood for, so took a wicked delight in this. One of my Primary 2 pupils who listened to the song, remembered it twenty years later and to put it in a cartoon in the *Guardian*. Nancy had settled down to do the *Guardian* crossword one day ... and was astonished to recognise herself in the cartoon beneath it. Karrie, then aged 6, had watched and listened intently as her teacher took the stage at Morning assembly. So many years later she could not remember the name of the teacher, but did remember the words – and that word – in the song. Teacher and former pupil, Karrie Fransman, met up at an Edinburgh Book Festival, and were delighted to share reminiscences. Recorded on *Rhyme and Reason*, 1990.

Don't Call Maggie a Cat

Don't call Maggie a Cat,
It's dreadful of you to say that,
For cats are soft and cats are warm,
Never did you any harm,
And it would cause the Cats alarm
If you called Maggie a Cat.

Don't call Maggie a Cow,
Or you'll get a terrible row,
For Cows are gentle, Cows are mild,
Cows give *milk* to feed a child,
And it would make the Cows so wild
if you called Maggie a Cow.

Don't call Maggie a Snake,
What an awful mistake you would make
A Snake just has ONE poisoned part,
His poisoned tongue, no poisoned heart,
And darlings, how the Snakes would smart
If you called Maggie a Snake.

Don't call Maggie a Bitch,
although your tongue may itch,
A Bitch may let her *puppy* roam...
but the pup would find his own way home,
And all the doggies' mouths would foam
if you called Maggie a Bitch.

June 1970, Thatcher, as Secretary of Sate for Education & Science, abolished universal free school milk.
Her son Mark got himself lost on a motoring rally in the Sahara. His rescue cost a lot of money.

So don't call Maggie a name.
It's a terribly hurtful game,
For those whose name you use for her
will not agree, will not concur,
Ye'll ruffle their feathers, ye'll stir their fur
The beasts are bound to complain

So don't call Maggie a Name!!

First published in the Guardian, www.guardian.co.uk, 05/09/08

Don't Call Maggie a Bitch Cartoon by © Karrie Fransman for the Guardian

LOVE, LIFE, AND LOSS

The Fairmer

A'm joost giein God a wee han
Tae win a bit food fae the lan,
A'm no really bothered the name o the God,
A'll turn a bit furr and A'll lift a wee clod,
For any Almichty that gies me the nod,
A'm juist giein God a wee han.

It's too big a job for juist wan
No maitter hoo tall he may stan,
Fan He's in the Wast Park fa's watchin the East,
Fan He's at the crops then faa's watchin the Beasts,
Fan He's at the hens, A say 'Faa's at the geese?'
That's me giein God a wee han.

He's no a bad boss noo, is God,
He lets ye maintain yer ain lod,
Bit times A jalouse he can be a bit fly,
Ah toil ower late, never take a lang lie,
An he lets me lod aa the cairts far ower high,
He's fond o me giein a han.

An sometimes A really must tell
A'd raither juist dae it masel,
For whilies A think his mind's no on the job,
A blooter he'll send or a gale he will lob,
Till the corn's lyin flat it wid mak a saint sob,
He still kens A'll gie him a han.

Then there's days at A feel lek a Laird,
When every job hes been squared,
A breeze ripples ower the ripening park,

I long ago ceased to believe in an Almighty Being managing Creation from above. I'd rather trust the World to folk who are closer to the earth that makes the Earth.

The Sun's on ma back an A'm hearin a lark,
Wi ma thoombs in ma weskit A hae tae remark,
That's me giein God a we han.

Wi ma thoombs in ma weskit A hae tae remark,
That's me giein God a we han.

Showing Cattle (© Johnston Collection)

THE MISTRESS — Nancy Nicolson

REFRAIN

Her eyes are dark, her breast is deep, That steals a wed-ded wumman's sleep, That tempts good men in-to her keep And will not let them free. The moon up-on her shoul-der gleams, That sir-en of the oce-an streams, Who whis-pers in a sea-man's dreams "No mist-ress have but me."

VERSES

My faith-er was a skee-ly skip-per, kind as he was brave, He claimed as fuend the tide and wind, as brither named the wave, His ves-sel she was clinker-built, stout and strong and sound, But they were taken by the sea, nor man nor board were found.

The Mistress

CHORUS

> Her eyes are dark, her breast is deep
> That steals a wedded wumman's sleep,
> That tempts good men into her keep

And will not let them free,
The moon upon her shoulder gleams,
That siren of the ocean streams
Who whispers in a seaman's dreams,
'No mistress have but me'.

My faither was a skeely skipper, kind as he was brave,
He claimed as freend the tide and wind, as brither named the wave,
  His vessel she was clinker-built, stout and strong and sound,
  But they were taken by the sea, nor man nor board were found.

    Her eyes are dark, her breast is deep...

My brither jined a merchantman to traivel foreign lands,
He smiled and said 'Don't worry' as my mither wrung her hands.
  In shorter than a twel-month she wrung her handkerchief,
  Wur Billy wis lost overboard, taen by yon brazen thief.

    Her eyes are dark, her breast is deep...

I widna coort a sailin lad, a welder is my man,
But he's gaen tae the ile-rigs an here in dreid I stan,
  I see an ancient omen, a sign o dule an hairm,
  I see the new moon sailin wi the auld moon in her airm

    Her eyes are dark, her breast is deep...

Recorded on *Rhyme and Reason*, 1990. After I wrote 'Who Pays the Piper?' I began to wonder on the event, musing on the fascination that the sea holds for men, like the irresistible hold of a Mistress. I considered generations who had gone to sea and faced its dangers, and the song 'The Mistress' formed in my mind. It speaks of a woman who thought she could avoid the pattern of tragedy. My Granny Stewart introduced me to the vision of 'the new moon with the auld moon in her arms'. I used to observe the phenomenon in the high clear Caithness skies. Granny sang me lines from the Ballad of Sir Patrick Spens. I reckon that's why the 'skeely skipper' phrase appeared.

THE MOON IN THE MORNING   Nancy Nicolson

INTRO

REFRAIN

The moon in the morn-ing still clings to the sky
Try-ing to tell me it's night,— The
moon in the morn-ing is tell-ing me lies, And
I see the moon in your eyes.—

VERSES

It was gold-en Sept-em-ber The first time we met— The
harv-est moon shone eve-ry-where,— It was
then that you told me you'd ne-ver for-got The
way the moon shone in my hair.—

The Moon in the Morning

CHORUS

> *The moon in the morning still clings to the sky*
> *Trying to tell me it's night,*
> *The moon in the morning is telling me lies,*
> *And I see the moon in your eyes.*

It was golden September the first time we met,
The harvest moon shone everywhere,
It was then that you told me you'd never forget
The way the moon shone in my hair.

The moon in the morning ....

The midwinter moon shone on new-fallen snow,
As I lay warm by your side,
I forgot the moon changes the ebb and the flow,
Forgot that the moon turns the tide.

The moon in the morning...

A new moon in April cut clear, cold and high,
New moons are lucky they say,
But this new moon meant two moons up there in your sky,
Now I see clear as the day.

The moon in the morning...

The moon in the morning still shines through my tears
Minding me ever on you,
And the tears of the moon they will shine through the years,
Her tears are the soft morning dew.

The moon in the morning...

In Summer in the North of Scotland, it stays very light, so late night and early morning run into each other. This song is the lament of a girl, out late with her lad, so late it became morning. And there was the moon still sailing in a summer-blue sky ... trying to tell her it was still day ... telling her lies!

DON'T WASTE MA TIME — Nancy Nicolson

INTRO.

Ta ra — ta ra ra!

REFRAIN

You can waste ma mon-ey, waste ma booze, These are things that I can choose to lose,

Waste ma mon-ey, waste ma booze, But don't waste my time ——— Cos I can

make more mon-ey, buy more booze, That's not what gives me the blues, Cos I can

make more mon-ey, Buy more booze, But can't make more time ———

VERSES

I earn the green-backs, save them too, They hit your fing-ers, slip right through,

Mon-ey nev-er sticks to you, You nev-er heard of Banks? And

than you go and ask a fave Of Bill and Bob and Tom and Dave, And

I pay back the cash they gave, And you re-ceive the thanks.———

Don't Waste Ma Time

You can waste ma money, waste ma booze,
Those are things that I can choose to lose,
Waste ma money, waste ma booze,
But don't waste ma time.

> Cos I can make more money, buy more booze
> That's not what gives me the blues
> *Cos I can make more money, buy more booze*
> But can't make more time.

I earn the greenbacks, save them too,
They hit your fingers, slip right through,
Money never sticks to you,
You never heard of banks?

> And then you go and ask a fave
> Of Bill and Bob and Tom and Dave,
> And I pay back the cash they gave
> And you receive the thanks.

You can waste ma money....

Now, honey, when you get the blues
A little booze is what to use,
But just remember whose is whose
When you go back for more,

> And then if you are feelin dry,
> I'll tell you, darlin, what to try,
> Go where the ocean meets the sky
> And drink your way to shore.

You can waste ma money...

This song is based on that volatile mixture: Men, Women, Drink and Money. Written probably early 1990s.

For 'Time is Money', so they say,
So if you waste ma cash away
I need more time to make more pay,
Time is money too,
   And if you've used up all ma dough
   I'll tell you, darlin, where to go,
   It's black and blazin down below
   With fire and brimstone too.

You can waste ma money, waste ma booze
Those are things that I can choose to lose
Waste ma money ... waste ma booze ...
But don't waste ma time!!

Nancy Nicolson Scottish Storytelling Centre (©Allan McMillan)

NEW BOOTS

Nancy Nicolson

INTRO.

REFRAIN

New Boots, grand and fine, New Boots, tanned and shin-y;
New Boots of sup-ple leath-er, New Boots for new weath-er

VERSES

1
I see sun and spring, — But my feet are wear-y
Would you dance and sing — Change your boots, my dear-ie.

2
Old boots tra-velled far, — Tra-velled far and stead-y
Stead-y, aye, but stiff; — Too stiff for this la-dy.

New Boots

CHORUS
New Boots, grand and fine,
New Boots, tanned and shiny,
New Boots of supple leather,
New boots for new weather.

I see sun and spring,
But my feet are weary,
Would you dance and sing
Change your boots, my dearie.

New Boots, grand and fine,

Old boots traveled far,
Traveled far and steady;
Steady, aye, but stiff;
Too stiff for this lady

New Boots, grand and fine,

Old boots kept out rain
Though the streets were running,
But their sturdy grain
Never let the sun in.

New Boots, grand and fine,

Old boots maun be cast,
Spare them no back-glancin;
Lay them by at last,
Little do they ken o dancing.

New Boots, grand and fine, (twice)

A song about taking a look at your life, and making a few changes. Recorded by Frankie Armstrong on *I Heard a Woman Singing* (1998).

THEY SENT A WUMMAN! Nancy Nicolson

A sent for the doc-tor, A te-le-phoned to-day,—— The doc-tor wis an aff—— a time a com-in——— A sent for the doc-tor, but sor-ry for tae say——— A doc-tor ne-ver came --- they sent a wum-man!——— But Ah let her—— make me bet-ter——— Then A asked her could she no—— get in-tae nurs-in?——— A sent for the doc-tor but when she went a-way—— A could-nae un-der-stand why she wis curs-in———

They Sent a Wumman

A sent for the doctor, A telephoned today,
The doctor wis an affa time a-comin,
Ah sent for the doctor, but sorry for tae say,
A doctor never came – they sent a wumman!
But Ah let her make me better,
Then A asked her could she no get intae nursin?
A sent for the doctor but when she went away,
A couldnae understan why she wis cursin.

A sent for the pilot, A telephoned today,
The pilot wis an affa time a-comin,
A sent for the pilot, but sorry for tae say,
A pilot never came – they sent a wumman!
An she roared off, an she soared off,
Then in she came an made a perfect landing,
But why she simply widnae juist hae been an air hostess
A've got tae say is past my understandin.

A sent for the polis, A telephoned today,
The polis wis an affa time a-comin,
Ah sent for the polis, but sorry for tae say,
A polis never came – they sent a wumman!
But she nabbed the boys that grabbed the
Payroll fae the office in the High Street,
But still A felt she should be telt it's no a lassie's job-
A widnae wint her on the beat in my street.

A sent for the fairmer, A telephoned today,
The fairmer wis an affa time a-comin,
A sent for the fairmer, but sorry for tae say,
A fairmer never came – they sent a wumman!

It is the song, or rather, whine, of a wee man who could not countenance women being employed in jobs he considered 'Men's Work' .

But her coos were, an her soos were.
The very best, the top o aa the biddin,
An aal A did wis ask her hed her faither steyed at hame?
The next A kent wis A wis in the midden.

So A prayed tae Goad Almichty, A prayed til him the day
… …The Good Lord wis an affa time a-comin …
A prayed til God Almichty and GLORI-GLORI-AY,
THE GREAT ALMICHTY CAME---- SHE WIS A WUMMAN!
An she viewed me, she 'How-d'ye do-ed' me,
Says, Ma lad, ye willnae listen, ye're no learnin,
So here's a little lesson, boy, ye're comin back again,
An next time as a wumman ye're returnin …'

Reprise first four lines – give it big licks on final
"THEY SENT A WUMMAN"

'Mrs God' – Cartoon © Denness Morton

A CAMEL — Nancy Nicolson

INTRO.

VERSES

cam-el shall pass throug the eye of a need-le more eas-i-ly, dear, it is said, Than a rich man shall en-ter the King dom of Hea-ven. When that poor old rich man is dead, he is dead, When that poor old rich man is dead So

The Camel and the Rich Man

A camel shall pass through the eye of a needle
More easily, dear, it is said,
Than a rich man shall enter the Kingdom of Heaven
When that poor old rich man is dead, he is dead,
When that poor old rich man is dead.

The Bible, Matthew 19.24: "It is easier for a camel to go through the eye of a needle than for a rich man to enter the kingdom of God." I fear that may not hold today. Rich men control so much, they can surely control their entry into the Heavenly Home.

So gather not riches to lay up in store,
The message is patently clear
That you never can claim your reward up in Heaven
If you've gone and claimed it down here, dear, down here,
If you've gone and claimed it down here.

So we sweat and we toil and grow old in the service
Of filling the other chaps' banks,
Then we stand on the stair and we smile at St Peter
And wait for our welcome and thanks, for our thanks,
We wait for our welcome and thanks.

Aye, there we are there at the top o the stair,
When Big Peter says, 'You huv tae shift,
For the likes o just you must step back in the queue
For the wans that came up in the lift, in the lift,
For the wans that came up in the lift'.

An there are the fat cats, as large, dear, as life,
And just when I'm starting to quote
From the Bible, on rich men and camels and needles,
This fat man says, 'Look at ma coat, ma good coat',
This fat man says, 'Look at ma coat!'

His coat was of camel, of camel's fine hair,
It was spun, it was woven and sewn,
Ay, and every strand, by some poor weaver's hand,
Through the eye of a needle had gone, it had gone,
Through the eye of a needle had gone.

If wished, repeat first verse

THE BRICKIE'S BALLAD   Nancy Nicolson

VERSES

It was early one May on a fine summer's day gaun ma messages tae Willie Low's, I raised up my eyes where the guys in the skies On the scaffolding stood as they posed I saw me a view of a bright rosy hue Ah couldnae get oot ae ma mind When his shirt left his breeks and I saw the baith cheeks O a braw barrie brickie's behind. And

REFRAIN

now that brickie's cleavage appears in aa ma dreams An I Follae ma feet doon tae Nicolson Street as I scan every cleavage that gleams For oh, that brickie's cleavage, It has my heart ensnared An among aa that glass I search for the memory O aa that the braw brickie bared

The Brickie's Ballad

It was early one May on a fine summer's day
Gaun ma messages tae Willie Low's,
I raised up my eyes where the guys in the skies
On the scaffolding stood an they posed.
I saw me a view of a bright rosy hue
Ah couldnae get oot ae ma mind,
When his shirt left his breeks and I saw the baith cheeks
O a braw barry brickie's behind.

CHORUS

    An now that brickie's cleavage
    Appears in aa ma dreams,
    An I follae ma feet doon tae Nicolson Street
    An I scan every cleavage that gleams,
    For oh, that brickie's cleavage,
    It has my heart ensnared,
    An among aa that glass I search for the ... memory
    O aa that the braw brickie bared.

An some were as crimson as peonies bright,
An some were a vivid maroon,
An some were like ivory, shinin sae white
They looked like baith sides o the moon.
    In summer each bum burnt reid in the sun,
December they aa turnt blue,
Noo Ah gaze and Ah blink for that bum o rose pink

Sometimes 'I' sometimes 'A': I – the first person singular, for Grammar buffs, I sing or write I, sometimes the Caithnss form A or Ah as seems appropriate, or as it sits on the tongue. You do what suits you.
I was resident singer at The Royal Oak Bar in Edinburgh in the early nineties when Edinburgh's Empire Theatre was being updated to create the glorious glass-fronted Edinburgh Festival Theatre in nearby Nicolson Street.
Many of the builders drank at the Royal Oak. I sometimes introduce the song as an 'Industrial Ballad'. The melody is based on that of 'The Sandy Bell's Man', in its turn a Bavarian folk tune.

An ah'm thinkin, Rob , could it be you?

An now that brickie's cleavage....

Noo at any excuse I am oot ae the hoose
Daein messages Ah dinnae need,
There's soup tae the ceiling an leeks up the lum
An beans, bacon, bananies an breid,
But never a glimpse huv Ah seen o him since,
An noo that the Empire is done,
Ma een are a wet, for the sun it has set
On the orbs that I wish I had won!

An now that brickie's cleavage....

For comic effect, use the name of a member of the audience. For a two-syllable name sing: *An I think, Robin, could it be you?*

Edinburgh Festival Theatre (©Allan McMillan)

THE KEEPINGSAKES
Nancy Nicolson

VERSES

His eyes were blue and bon-ny and his smile was kind and free, He
gave to me the Keeping sakes be-fore he went to sea. He
left a lock of curl-ing hair, a peart-y pin for me to wear, And
all the sil-ver mus-ic of the song he sang for me.

REFRAIN

The Song is what I loved him for, dear-est boy and best, It
sings with-in my mem-or-y, it beats with-in my. And
if there is a lad that you love bet-ter than the rest,
See if you can tune in-to his song.

The Keepingsakes

His eyes were blue and bonnie and his smile was kind and
free, He gave to me the Keepingsakes before he went to sea,
He left a lock of curling hair, a pearly pin for me to wear,
And all the silver music of the song he sang to me.

The hair as dark and curling and it wound around my heart.
It tighter still and tighter grew til Life was like to part,
I took a knife to cut the strand, it fell so soft across my hand,
And so I lost the locket that the Sailor left to me.

I wore the pearly pin upon a scarf about my throat,
One morning as I fastened it I marveled for to note,
The pearl became a salty tear that left my eye all in a blear,
And so I lost the pretty pin the Sailor left to me.

The Song is what I loved him for, dearest boy and best,
It sings within my memory, it beats within my breast,
And if there is a lad that you love better than the rest,
See if you can tune into his song.

Repeat first verse if you wish

This song was written in the late 1980s. It is for my dear friend's man. He was on his last trip deep-
sea. Geordie never came home. Always remembered with love. Recorded on *Rhyme and Reason*,
1990.

IF I DIE — Nancy Nicolson

If I Die

CHORUS

> *'If I die', said the man tae his dear little wife,*
> *As he stood and he looked oot the windae,*
> *'IF!' said his wife, 'by ma sowl, by ma life,*
> *The wonder wid be if ye DIDNAE'*

'If I die,' he still said, 'if I die and I'm dead,
Wid the day still follow the morning?'
'When ma ain jo, when ye dee an ye go,
Dae ye think that the world wid stop turnin?'

'If I die', said the man........

'If I die,' he still said, 'if I die and I'm dead,
Wid the Moon an the Stars keep their places?'
'When ma ain jo, when ye dee an ye go,
dae ye think they wid cover their faces?'

'If I die', said the man........

'If I die,' he still said, 'if I die and I'm dead,
Up tae Heivin d'ye think God wid heft me?'
'When, ma ain jo, when ye dee an ye go,
Ah'll be left here wi naeb'dy tae fecht wi'.

'If I die', said the man........

When I sing it I repeat the last two lines, You may choose to do anything else to underline the unexpected ending.

Written probably 2008 or 2009. The idea for this song grew from a conversation wi ma Mam when I was about 12. I had made some point saying... 'If I die...' Mam cocked her head to one side, looked deep into my eyes, and said ... 'IF ye die!!'

Then her eyes filled wi tears, said 'Thae fifty fine years,
It wis only yersel that A lay wi.
When ma ain jo, when ye dee an ye go,
Sees yer haan, boy, for A'm comin wi ye'.

FLAGS

CLAN BEAG

Nancy Nicolson

REFRAIN 1 (to follow Verses 1 & 3)

Un-der-neath the moon,
in a-mong the dunes,
We are e-vil pee-die dee-vils, wick-ed, ill-tricked an sly, Clan
Beag an Don-al Mac-kay.

REFRAIN 2 (to follow Verses 2 & 4)

Un-der-neath the moon,
in a-mong the dunes, We
stir the tide an spin the wea-ther, We weave the cloth of Life to-geth-er,
Or-der of Mac-kay.

VERSES

Più Lento

And then we make Flaws when we wish Where fish an fowl an
Folk fall through, We are Clan Beag of Don-al Dhu

Clan Beag

CHORUS 1
Underneath the moon, in among the dunes
We are evil peedie deevils,
wicked, ill-tricked an sly,
Clan Beag an Donal Mackay.

CHORUS 1
Underneath the moon, in among the dunes
We stir the tide an spin the weather,
We weave the cloth of Life together,
Order of Mackay.

An then we make flaws where we wish
Where fish an fowl an folk fall through,
We are Clan Beag of Donal Dhu.

Underneath the moon ... (1)

An then we make loops that are loose
Where hoose an haven fill wi rue,
We are Clan Beag of Donal Dhu.

Underneath the moon ... (2)

An then we make tears in the side
Where tide and pride will all fall through,
We are Clan Beag of Donal Dhu.

Underneath the moon ... (1)

An when we create a wee spark
The dark wi blazin lowes is shot through,
We are Clan Beag of Donal Dhu.

Underneath the moon ... (2)

From Gaelic: clan – family, beag – small. This song, like the next five songs, was written in 1996 for George Gunn's play 'Flags', the story of the flagstone quarry at Castlehill, Dunnett in Caithness. *Clan Beag* were the tribe o peedie folk that were reputed to live among the dunes at Dunnet. I picture them similar to trolls or mischievious fairy folk. Their job was to spin from sand the ropes that hold Orkney in place so that it will not drift away into the Northern ocean.
They were magical creyturs, authors of the bad events that befell the Quarry owner. They delivered rough justice. Their Chief and Master was Donal Dhu Mackay, a defrocked priest. Traill House was the Quarry owner's mansion. When it went up in flames it was Clan Beag that created the spark .

Flagstone Quarry (© Johnson Collection)

Who Could Endure?

(Song of the Dispossessed of Sutherland)

From blazing thatch to icy shore,
Who could endure, who could endure?
With what we wear and nothing more,
Who could endure?
> The walk was long, mo ghaoil mo chridh,
> Sleep til dawning,
> We will be strong, mo ghaoil mo chridh,
> In this new day.

I fear to close my frightened eyes,
Who could endure, who could endure?
I hear her voice, my mother's cries,
Who could endure?

Many of the workers in the quarry at Castlehill on the Pentland shore were cleared people of Sutherland, those who, rather than go to Glasgow or across the Atlantic, travelled on foot to North Kaitness. This was the song of the migrants as they arrived after their sorry journey.

But we survive, *mo ghaoil mo chridh,*
And our children
We are alive, *mo ghaoil mo chridh,*
In this new day.

His hair is wet, my little son,
His feet are sore and bleeding.
I hold him close my little one,
Past all heeding,
> But we are strong and when we rest
> We will gather
> The strength to take us through the test
> Of this new day.

There is no roof above my head,
Who could endure, who could endure? Cold stones to make
my children's bed,
Who could endure?
> But with those stones I build a wall,
> We will gather
> A branch , a plaid to shelter all
> In this new day.

O for my own, my sheltered strath,
Who could endure, who could endure?
To leave the roaring ocean's wrath,
Who could endure?
> That time is past, that day is done,
> Bed and bohan,
> They must be made, they must be won,
> In this new day.

Repeat verse 1

WAN MORE COWG   Nancy Nicolson

INTRO.

Na na na na na na! ——

REFRAIN

Choost wan more cowg in wan more wheel, Wan more dowg a-blow a weel-shod heel,

Wan more cowg in wan more wheel, An plen-ty stand-in wait-in.

VERSES

Wai - ai - tin! For e meenad when a cowld hand slips,

Wait-in for a tired man's blun-der   Wai - ai - tin! For a

meenad when a worn boot trips   An some chiel's feet is un-der.

Wan More Cowg

CHORUS
> *Choost wan more cowg in wan more wheel,*
> *Wan more dowg ablow a weel-shod heel,*
> *Wan more cowg in wan more wheel*
> An plenty stannin waitin.

Wai-ai-tin! for e meenad when a cowld han slips,
Waitin for a tired man's blunder,
Wai-ai-tin! for e meenad when a worn boot trips,
An some *chiel's feet* is under.

> *Choost Wan more cowg ...*

Wai-ai-tin! for e meenad when e bogey jolts,
An some chiel hesna seen id.
Wai-ai-tin! for e flag at slips agenst e bolts,
Wi some chiel's haan atween id.

> *Choost Wan more cowg ...*

Wai-ai-tin! for e meenad when a weet back bends,
An pain shots lek an arrow.
Wai-ai-tin! for e meenad when a work life ends,
A broken man tomorrow.

> *Choost Wan more cowg ...*

The flagstone industry was hard and heavy, with a high number of injuries and casualties. There was always someone waiting to take on the job of a man who was injured and sacked.

James Traill, Ah gied Ye Ma Son

CHORUS

    James Traill, A gied ye ma son,

    James Traill, ma wan son, ma beeg an ma bonnie ,

    James Traill, A gied ye ma son,

    An fit did ye do wi him?

Manhandling flagstones, often 7 feetx5 feet, was a hard, heavy and dangerous job. The men moved a flag by 'waltzing' it across the ground on its two lower corners. Many workers wore out their bones and muscles. Many others suffered desperate injuries. This song is in the voice of a mother.

Could dance as licht as any wan,
An oot-run any ither,
Now waaks doon e rod lek a bent owld man
Til a broken-herted mither.

James Traill, A gied ye ma son

Wid play his whistle til e beat,
An heel-an-toe he'd caper,
Now shauchles sore on broken feet
Wi fingers frail as paper.

James Traill, A gied ye ma son

His smile wid charm e very birds,
His laugh lek crystal clinkin,
His broo now dark wi silent words,
No future worth e thinkin.

James Traill, A gied ye ma son

An soon e quarries they will go
Forgotten in their goin,
But there is wan thing that I know
No grief will I be showin,

James Traill, A gied ye ma son

COLD COMFORT   Nancy Nicolson

INTRO.

La la la la la la ——

REFRAIN

I am left with cold com-fort, a stone in my heart, I am left with Cold Comfort to keep —— I am left with Cold Com-fort, a stone in my heart, As hard as Win-ter deep. ——

VERSES

Poco piu mosso

And the day dawned fair in the morn-ing —— And the sun shone bright at noon, —— But the sun that set in its blaz—ing red was cold as a mid—night moon. ——

Cold Comfort

CHORUS
> *I am left with cold comfort, a stone in my heart,*
> *I am left with Cold Comfort to keep,*
> *I am left with Cold Comfort, a stone in my heart*
> *As hard as Winter deep.*

And the day dawned fair in the morning
And the sun shone bright at noon,
But the sun that set in its blazing red
Was cold as a midnight moon.

> *I am left with cold comfort, ...*

With a cold stone field for a dowry
I was wedded to James Traill,
But his golden guineas they built a wall
As high as a cold stone Jail.

> *I am left with cold comfort, ...*

Now the babe I bore in such labour
Lies in the clay and dead,
And the womb should furnish warmth and life
Lies cold as a flagstone bed.

> *I am left with cold comfort, ...*

So you wept a wee tear for Janet Traill? Dinna worry, Caithness toffs are hardy toffs – she went on to have nine of a family. This song for George Gunn's 1996 community play *Flags* is in the voice of Janet Traill, wife of quarry-owner James Traill and daughter of John Sinclair who sold Traill the Castlehill quarry in Caithness . There were some who believed she was a pawn in the deal for the quarry. Janet dearly wanted children, but when after a long wait she had a son, her baby died in infancy. In the play she stands broken-hearted on the shore to sing the song.

Good Intentions

JT – Quarry owner James Traill

JT: My intentions are good intentions,
    Of the noblest, of the fairest.
Workers: Yur intenshins ur good intenshins,
    An we ken fit e rod til Hell is paved wi.

JT: I gave you work, I gave you labour,
    Of the noblest, of the fairest.
Workers: Back-breakin work an stolen labour,
    An we ken fit e rod til Hell is paved wi.

JT: I gave you homes, I gave you shelter,
    Of the noblest, of the fairest.
Workers: Ye gave us stons, we beelt e shelter,
    An we ken fit e rod til Hell is paved wi.

JT: I gave you food and coals to warm you,
    Of the noblest, of the fairest.
Workers: Ye sellt us coal at gey warm prices,
    An we ken fit e rod til Hell is paved wi.

JT: A thriving trade, a wealthy county,
    Of the noblest, of the fairest.
Workers: We gave the toil, Ye took the bounty,
    An we ken fit e rod til Hell is paved wi.

JT: But my intentions are good intentions,
    Of the noblest, of the fairest.

Workers: Yur Intenshins ur good intenshins,
    An we ken fit e rod til Hell is paved wi.

James Traill quarry-owner, was a boss of the same tenor as contemporary mill-and mine-owners of 19th century. Entirely secure in his role as a pillar of the community, he regarded himself as a great benefactor and generous employer. At a formal dinner he talked of his role, and proudly stated, "My intentions are good Intentions", missing the irony of being a producer of flagstones – paving stones – and the old saw "the road to hell is paved with good intentions." The song is a dialogue between Traill, in Queen's English, and his Caithness workers in native Kaitness, speaking in the strong dialect of the county. The successful business exported paving stones all over the globe – Wellington, Montevideo. They paved the Strand in London and built St Pancras Station. Traill operated a tack system, so the workers were totally in thrall to him. All the money he paid them he got back when they bought provisions. The quarry workers had to build their own houses – not from good Caithness flags, but from the ballast from the three-masted schooners that transported the good stuff out of Castlehill harbour.

WAR AND PEACE

THE EAGLE AND THE BEAR   Nancy Nicolson

INTRO.
La la la la la la la la la la la la la!—

REFRAIN

Once there was an Eag-le,— Once there was a Bear,—
Once there was a Lit-tle Li-on in be-tween the pair,—
"Nyaa-aah!" went the Eag-le, "Grrrr!" went the Bear—
"Mammy!" went the Lit-tle Li-on in be-tween the pair.—

    * Pitch indeterminate

VERSES

The Eag-le had a rock-et, the Bear had a sub, But
neith-er one could reach the oth-er one, now there's the rub. The
subs and the rock-ets could reach as far as where?
Just as far as the Lit-tle Li-on in be-tween the pair. —

The Eagle and the Bear

CHORUS
Once there was an Eagle, once there was a Bear,
Once there was a Little Lion in between the pair,
Yee-eek went the Eagle, Grr-rrr went the Bear,
'Mammy!' went the Little Lion in between the pair.

The Eagle had a rocket, the Bear had a sub,
But neither one could reach the other one, now there's the rub.
The subs and the rockets could reach as far as where?
Just as far as the Little Lion in between the pair.

Once there was......

The Eagle scratched his feathers, the Bear tore his hair,
Till they found them a solution that they both thought fair.
The Eagle planted rockets on the Little Lion's face,
the Bear ran his subs around the little Lion's place.

Once there was......

We used tae stamp a little Lion on an eggie's shell,
To show that it was fresh and clean and good and sound as well.
This eggshell island has been conned and foiled,
By the rockets we'll be scrambled, by the subs we will be boiled.

Once there was.......

Written in the 1980s. My simple peedie heid sometimes needs to view big problems in a simple way. Verse three refers to the decision of the British Egg Marketing Authority to stamp a wee lion on eggs to signify freshness and quality. Recorded on *Rhyme and Reason*, 1990.

The Little Lion used tae be a power tae himsel,
Consignin half the world tae British Rule or else tae Hell.
Noo, Puir thing, he plays a second fiddle,
He's no a bloody Lion, He's a Piggy-in-the-middle.

Once there was.......

Nancy Nicolson at the Edinburgh Folk Club ©Allan McMillan

WOE IS ME

Nancy Nicolson

Woe is me to be be-side the sea-side,

Woe is me to be be-side the sea

Woe be-tide the toe that tae the tide does go It's

tol-al-ly ta-boo toe-base to be As-

-sur-an-ces are showered up-on the shore-line, But

I say B N F's an F N B Don't

let your son or daughter pad-dle in the Heav-y Water, There's

sure tae be mair cae-si-um than sea. Don't

let your son or daughter pad-dle in the Heav-y Water, There's

sure tae be mair cae-si-um than sea.

Woe Is Me

Woe is me to be beside the seaside,
Woe is me to be beside the sea,
Woe betide the toe that tae the tide does go,
It's totally taboo toe-bare to be,

Assurances are showered upon the shoreline,
But I say BNF's an F-N-B, ...British Nuclear Fuel
Don't let your son or daughter paddle in the Heavy Water,
There's sure tae be mair caesium than sea.

> Don't let your son or daughter paddle in the Heavy Water
> There's sure tae be mair caesium than sea.

Woe is me to be beside the seaside,
Woe is me tae be beside the sea,
Woe the Little Earth, Oh the little Worth,
Plutonium's valued more than air or sea.

I do not want mutations for relations.
Or incandescent lovers at my knee.
I'm only taking issue for to save my aching tissue.
Fae aa ra errors in ra err an sea.

> I'm only taking issue for to save my aching tissue.
> Fae aa ra errors in ra err an sea.

For all the sparkling shores around Dounreay on the Pentland Firth.

NUCLEAR LOVE SONG

Nancy Nicolson

INTRO

VERSE

Dar-ling, you are rad-i-ant, You've nev-er looked like this be-fore.

Cheeks a-flame, eyes a glow, My heart is melt-ing on the floor... at your feet...

Dar-ling, you are rad-i-ent In in-can-des-cent hue, And

just be-fore you va-por-ise, Look! I'm ir-rad-i-at-ing too!

Nuclear Love Song

Darling you are radiant
You've never looked like this before,
Cheeks aflame eyes aglow,
My heart is melting on the floor ... at your feet.
Darling you are radiant
In incandescent hue
And just before you vaporise
Look, ... I'm irradiating too.

E MAN AT MUFFED IT — Nancy Nicolson

E Man At Muffed Id

CHORUS

> *A'm the man at Muffed id. A'm the man at boobed,*
> *A'm the man at loast the radioactive tube,*
> *So A'll ask ma process workers til tell me faar id's geen,*
> *For if id took a dander, surely hid was seen!*

Wullie the crofter, could it be you?
Naa, id wisna wan A took. A took two,
Wan hes peened ma gate shut, the ither's in e park,
Hids gran fine glow takes me safely through e dark.

> *A'm the man...*

Angie e fisherman, tell e truth til me.
Naa id wisna wan a took. A took three,
Wan is on ma nets, id makes a damn fine float,
E ither two's a microwave oaven in ma boat.

> *A'm the man...*

Fa's yin skookin oot an through e door?
Id's Hector, e whusky maker, A took four,
A run ma barley bree through e tubie til distil,
A sell the maut til ye beys, an at's how ye get fill.

> *A'm the man...*

In Nuclear Caithness Atoms are good news.
They brocht his jobs and money we'd be stupid til refuse,
So now we've Nuclear Fish, fine Atomic Coos,
Plutonium-coated People an Radio-active Booze!

Recorded on *Rhyme and Reason*, 1990.

A'm the man...

Yes, A'm the man at muffed id, A'm yur buey at boobed,

A wonder will they fin their radio-active tube?

Bit there's no goan be no search, nor any beeg to-do,..

Cos e storeman says he's loast all his Geiger-counters too –

.... A-a-an.... .....A'm the man.... surely id was seen !!!

In 1958 Caithness the 'Fast Reactor Establishment Dounreay' was the pride and joy of the United Kingdom Atomic Energy Authority, on the Pentland Firth shores, ten miles West of Thurso. The huge dome was christened FRED.

We natives were invited to visit and marvel at the exhibition the UKAEA made in 1958. They had even produced a wee booklet, 'A Glossary of Atomic Terms' (GOAT?) and proudly introduced it saying, 'This book has been written by those of us inside the Nuclear industry so that those outside may understand what we do.' I am sorry I have to write this from memory as I have lost my copy. If anyone out there has one, I'd love to have a look!

There were some stunning acronyms:

'MCA: A Maximum Credible Accident is what would happen if all fail-safes on the site failed. It is a condition of licensing that this would cause no significant harm to the few public.'

Well, ma dears, that is reassuring, isn't it? Or is it? I was talking at the time to 'someone who knows' and he put me right. 'Public?' he said, 'There is no public in Caithness. There are Dounreay employees and Dounreay employees' families. There are Dounreay suppliers and Dounreay suppliers' families. That leaves precious few public.'

Then he explained the particular meaning of 'significant' in 'significant harm'. 'Significant? In any public disaster the numbers of dead are commuted as a percentage of the entire population of the UK. If the whole of Caithness were wiped off the face of the Earth the numbers would not be significant in that context.'

Oh, dearie me, not so reassuring.

And what about MUF?

'MUF: Materials Unaccounted For is the difference between the book inventory and the physical inventory of radio-active materials on site. This is a management aid, and not a measure of actual loss, or gain.'

Whoops, MUF is about as reassuring as MCA!

There were at least two instances of a radio-active isotope going a-missing.

There was lamentable security on gates. The workforce was made up in large part of crofters and fishermen, some of whom were still plying their original trades ... dressed in Dounreay issue first-class rubber boots, overalls and various bits of gear and implements.

The song 'E Man at Muffed Id' practically wrote itself.

Sometimes I write or say 'E Man', at other times 'The Man'.

It depends on the company and county wherein I find myself.

Dounreay Nuclear Power plant

GULF STREAM   Nancy Nicolson

Gulf Stream

In Scotland we had a Gulf Stream ran right up our back,
Across the top an doon the front an it was luvvly,
But noo, God preserve us, no wonder we're nervous,
As doon tae the sea we go waaddlin,
Ower sands that can spark and glow green in the dark,
For scintillatin radiatin paddlin.

In Scotland we had a Gulf Stream ran right up our back,
Across the top an doon the front an it was luvvly.
Fae Sellafield, that's Windscale, there's mair than tide and winds sail,
Mair danger in the water than droonery,
Ye've heerd aboot coals tae Newcastle I'm shair
It takes radioactivity tae Doun-e-ray

In Scotland we had a Gulf Stream ran right up our back,
Across the top an doon the front an it was luvvly.
It's o such a blessing our tidelines caressing,
It flows round our beaches, a-warming them,
No word of the hot spots no word of alarm,
No mention that the flowing tide is harming them.

In Scotland we had a Gulf Stream ran right up our back,
Across the top an doon the front an it was luvvly.
While doon in Westminister, are men sleek an sinister,
Who always eat cake, never gru-u-el,
Who run the experiments, but never run the risk,
Of ever getting near to nuclear fuel.

I have had someone ask me why my songs are so cynical. I had to reply that I have no alternative. The cynicism of Government and Authority requires a response in kind. This song was triggered after there was a bad leak of radio-activity from Windscale, the Nuclear station in the North West of England. What was the official response? They renamed the facility 'Sellafield'. Did they think we'd imagine it was not the same place, the same station, with the same risks? And I pay tribute to Mrs Maggie Scott, Geography teacher at Wick High School in the Fifties, who taught us so well to appreciate and understand the Gulf Stream and its role in warming Scotland's back.

In Scotland we had a Gulf Stream ran right up our back,
Across the top an doon the front an it was luvvly.
The Gulf Stream we're singing of, so warm and benign,
Is carrying a load of disa-aster
But I tell you stranger, it's nothing to the danger
Of Government that rules as a master.

And so when I vote. I'll take them by the throat.
It's MY vote, and I ken how to cast her
When YOU GO TO VOTE. just take them by the throat.
It's YOUR vote, and YOU ken how to cast her.

Gone With the Wind (Poster for the Socialist Worker by Bob Light and John Houston)

DO NOTHING   Nancy Nicolson

INTRO

Da da da da da da da! ——

REFRAIN

All you have to do is do no-thing,—— No-thing, —— no-thing. All you have to do is do no-thing,— And YOU will bring us the Bomb!——

VERSES

Big Maggie Thatcher can't do it her-self, It would stay in the box, it would stay on the shelf, Big Mag-gie Thatch-er can't do it her-self, She can't do a thing without you. AND ALL

Do Nothing

CHORUS
> *All you have to do is do nothing,*
> *Nothing, nothing.*
> *All you have to do is do nothing,*
> *And YOU will bring us the Bomb!*

Big Maggie Thatcher can't do it herself,
It would stay in the box, it would stay on the shelf,
Big Maggie Thatcher can't do it herself,
She can't do a thing without you.

> *All you have to do ...*

Big Ronnie Reagan can't do it alone
Or the poor little Bomb would be staying at home,
Big Ronnie Reagan can't do it alone,
He can't do a thing without you.

> *All you have to do ...*

Maggie and Ronnie, that wonderful crew,
They are lost without me, they are lost without you
Maggie and Ronnie, that wonderful crew,
They can't do a thing without you.

An iconic image of the 1980s was the chilling parody of the 'Gone With the Wind' poster of Clark Gable and Vivien Leigh set against a blazing Tara. The parody had Ronald Reagan's Rhett sweeping Margaret Thatcher's Scarlett into his arms against a looming mushroom cloud. We will indeed be 'Gone With the Wind' if the war-mongering cowboys have their wicked way. One element of certain political songs is their inbuilt use-by date.

Sadly, as at the cinema, if you watch long enough the film, or song, comes round again. This time, admittedly, it was with a different cowboy, and verily, George Bush did seduce the doe-eyed Blair and sweep him into his ARMS..... for Iraq. Someone must have made a poster for that too. It is in our gift to let them get off with it. All we have to do is to do nothing. I wrote this in the mid-80s. It did not get as many airings as I would have liked, for I was chained into the 60-hour week necessary to be a teacher/trade-unionist at the time. I therefore

have to number myself among those who did nothing. Well, who's got time to save the world with thirty-three Primary 3 sum books to correct? This song was published 2008 in *Now More than Ever, Here More than Anywhere, 50 Years of Scottish Songs for Nuclear Disarmament*, edited by Penny Stone

THE CRAWS CAA'D 'COLLATERAL'   Nancy Nicolson

INTRO.

La la la la la la la la!

REFRAIN

Oh the craws caa'd 'Col-lat-er-al, Col-lat-er-al,—
Col-lat-er-al,' And the craws caa'd 'Col-lat-er-al'—
And The Gen-er-al's on The T. V.

VERSES

Now please tell me, Gen-er-al, how can it be That
wo-men and bab-ies lie dead?— 'We weren't
aim-ing at them, they just got in the way, They're col-
lat-er-al dam-age', he said—

The Craws Caa'd 'Collateral'

Oh the craws caa'd 'Collateral,
Collateral, collateral'
The craws caa'd 'Collateral',
And The General's on the TV.

Now please tell me, General, how can it be
That women and babies lie dead?
'We weren't aiming at them, they just got in the way,
They're collateral damage', he said,

And the craws caa'd, 'Collateral, ... '
An the wee dug barked for his boy.

The boy he is gane wi his Mammy and Daddy,
Their haill life piled on a cairt,
He cairries his bundle o gear on his back,
The heaviest burden, his hert.

And the craws caa'd, 'Collateral, ... '
And Irene. she ran for the wuids.

She hid in the trees and she trembled wi fear,
She stood on a twig an it cracked,
Too frichtened tae answer the harsh 'Who goes there?'
And a bullet tore intae her back.

During the war in Kosovo in the late 1990s, TV war-correspondent John Simpson presented a nightly programme from Pristina. It was a war with high civilian casualties – not a phrase liked by governments or military on any side. They preferred to call it "Collateral Damage". Each evening's programme began with a signature recording of crows cawing and one wee bark from a dog. As John reported the big events of war each day he also drew searing little cameos from everyday life – or death – as it happened. I created a scenario for the wee dog barking, but the other scenes were incidents reported: the wee girl shot in the back; the man weeping as he left in a bus, his parents left behind. I wrote the song at the same time as the events.

And the craws caa'd, 'Collateral, ... '
And the big strong man, he wept.

His Faither an Mither were faur ower frail
Tae traivel tae some unkan place,
They stood, prood an plain, as his bus drew awa,
An the tears burnt intae his face

And the craws caa'd, 'Collateral, ... '
There's a bairn on the road lyin dead.

In Vietnam and Bosnia, Afghanistan,
It was always the innocent bled,
There's a Warrior standing, a gun in his han,
And a bairn on the road lying dead.

And the craws caa'd, 'Collateral, ... '
There's a bairn on the road lyin dead.

Nancy Nicolson Scottish Storytelling Centre (©Allan McMillan)

BOYS AND TOYS — Nancy Nicolson

INTRO.

VERSES

1. Geord-ie Geord-ie Bush Bush, Geord-ie Geord-ie Bush Bush,
Geord-ie Geord-ie Bush Bush Had a ter-ri-ble toy-box,
It was full of bombs and guns Blood-y great e-norm-ous ones
Duck, ma dar-lin, here it comes, Geord-ie Bush's toy - box

2. Sad-dam Sad-dam Hus-sein, Sad-dam Sad-dam Hus-sein,
Sad-dam Sad-dam Hus-sein was a ter-ri-ble ty-rant,
Might is right, the des-pot said, Wrung his peo-ple till they bled,
If they dis-a- gree, they're dead, Sad-dam was a ty- rant.

* Optional :- SPOKEN

Boys and Toys

to the Gaelic air "Mire Mire Miuch Miuch"

1) Geordie Geordie Bush Bush, Geordie Geordie Bush Bush,
   Geordie Geordie Bush Bush, Had a terrible toy-box,
   It was full of bombs and guns, Bloody great enormous ones,
   Duck, ma darlin, here it comes, Geordie Bush's toy-box.

2) Saddam Saddam Hussein. Saddam Saddam Hussein,
   Saddam Saddam Hussein, Was a terrible tyrant
   Might is right, the despot said, Wrung his people till they bled,
   If they disagree, they're dead, Saddam was a tyrant.

3) Geordie Geordie bush Bush, Geordie Geordie Bush Bush,
   Geordie Geoirdie bush Bush, Saw elections coming.
   What a chance, upon my soul, Wartime leaders top the poll,
   Let the tanks and missiles roll, Gotta stay in the White House.

4) Tony Tony Blair Blair, Tony Tony Blair Blair,
   Tony Tony Blair Blair, Longed to play wi the big boys
   Bambi was a little 'dear', Now he had to make it clear
   Tony was a force to fear, Out to play with the big boys.

5) Tony calling Dubya, Tony calling Dubya,
   Tony calling Dubya, Come and see MY toy-box,
   I have regiments galore Primed and polished for a war,
   Take them, Georgie. Here they are, Have ... the British Army!

I wrote this at Easter 2004, thinking of Gordon Gentle and his mother Rose. People familiar with the canon of Scottish songs will recognise my homage to other writers; Vs 6: Now's the Day and Now's the Hour... from 'Scots Wha Hae', by Robert Burns. Vs 7: You will soldier far away... from 'The Scottish Soldier' by Andy Stewart.
ref verse 4: The newly-elected Blair was likened to Bambi due to his wide-eyed, lolloping style.

6) Stand ... to attention! Stand ... to attention!
   Stand ... to attention!, Says the sergeant major.
   Now's the day and now's the hour, See the front o battle lower,
   To keep two parasites in power, Here's your marching orders.

7) Kiss Goodbye to Mammy, Kiss Goodbye to Mammy,
   Kiss Goodbye to Mammy, Bonnie Scottish Soldi
   You will soldier far away, You will fight in mony a fray,
   You ken the price that you may pay, You're the Flower of Scotland.

8) Ma laddie is a hero, Ma laddie is a hero,
   Ma laddie is a hero, Oot there on the front line.
   Silently I pace the floor,Secretly ma hert is sore,
   Ah dread the knock upon the door, Laddie's on the front line.

   !!! !!! !!! (knock, knock, knock)

9) Sumb'dy's at the door, Ma, Sumb'dy's at the door, Ma,
   Sumb'dy's at the door, Ma, ...He says... he's fae... the Army**...**

   (Pause ... ... cue the Last Post)

George W Bush and Tony Blair – Cartoon © Steve Bell for the *Guardian*

TONY B-LIAR

Nancy Nicolson

INTRO.

VERSE

Ton-y B Li-ar, yer breeks are on fi-re, Ye tried tae con-vince us, ye could-nae, There wis no smok-ing gun, on-ly your smok-ing bum, Noo yer erse is oot o the win-dae!

Tony B-Liar

Tony B Liar, yer breeks are on fire,
Ye tried tae convince us, ye couldnae,
There wis no smoking gun, only your smoking bum,
Noo yer erse is oot o the windae!

This was written around 2006. There are occasions when disparate ideas come together. The song is a stew of these three:

> A *Guardian* misprint of Blair's name as Bliar: *... B-liar ... how true*
> The old playground taunt: 'Liar, liar, your pants are on fire!'
> And the colourful Glasgow judgment that a person has no chance: 'Yer erse is oot ae the windae'.

It's the shortest song I have written.

The publication of the Chilcott Report in July 2016 has proved us all right. There were no weapons of mass destruction. Blair sent countless young men to kill innocents, and to die in a war that was based on a lie.

A FREE FLAG · Nancy Nicolson

REFRAIN

Come join the re-gi-ment, meet all the boys, line up for your share of the fun Live the ad-ven-ture and taste all the joys of spark-ling snow-scapes and sun. Free food and free hous-ing, two fine free suits, You've made it, you've land-ed you're laugh-in And your own Free one-gun sal-ute, And a Free Flag and a cof-fin

VERSES

Learn free trans-fer-ab-le skills, Com-put-ing and dash-ing brav-a-do, Leap-ing through for-ests and ski-ing down hills In the re-gi-ment, your El-do-rad-o So what is the job like? Just ask me, I know, Sun-shine comes with land mines as stand-ard And hope that they've got bod-y ar-mour for you When in-to an am-bush you've wan-dered.

*Optional:- SPOKEN

A Free Flag

CHORUS

Come join the regiment, meet all the boys,
Line up for your share of the fun,
Live the adventure and taste all the joys,
Of sparkling snowscapes and sun.

Free food and free housing, two fine free suits,
You've made it, you've landed, you're laughin,
And your own free one-gun salute
And a free flag and a coffin.

Learn *free* transferable skills,
Computing and dashing bravado,
Leaping through forests and ski-ing down hills
In the regiment, your Eldorado

So what is the job like? Just ask me, I know,
Sunshine comes with landmines as standard,
And hope that they've got body armour for you
When into an ambush you've wandered.

Come join the ...

Your *new* boss and commander, the Queen
Has generals for to direct you,
Not quite as committed as they might have been
Provisioning for to protect you,

For it's no body armour, the wrong kind of boots,
Rifles that foul up with sand,
Motors with engines not worth a blue toot,
And grenades that blow up in your hand.

Come join the ...

Written in 2006. A song I had to write in response to a Government Army recruiting campaign on TV and in Schools. Treat the first section as chorus, or if that makes it too long, start and finish with it.

Think, bonnie laddie, think once and think twice,
Think for your wife and your mother
Think of the consequence, think of the price,
Your future, your children, your brother.
> Just picture a graveside, the troops at their station
> Your wife and your mother in tears,
> Your children, they stumble in grey desolation
> Beneath the full weight of their fears.

Come join the...

Anthony Blair and Wee Geordie Bush
Need you for their cannon fodder.
Just give their recruiting the push,
They can't make a war wi no sodgers.
> Dubya and Tony, we ken the whole story,
> The game is up, lads, we've tumbled,
> The wars are just for your own profit and glory
> So fecht them yoursels boys, you're rumbled.

Come join the...

Two Boys in Uniform ((© Johnston Collection)

Ev'ry Little Sparrow

I-if ev'ry little sparrow flapped his wing, wing, wing
At the same same time. what a thing thing thing,
If ev'ry little sparrow flapped his wing,
What a great gale that would be.

> Flap together with the whole wide world,
> Whole wide world, whole wide world,
> Flap together with the whole wide world,
> What a great, great Gale!

I woke up early Monday 18 Dec 2006, and this just poured out.

I-if ev'ry little beetle stamped his foot, foot, foot
At the same same time, they came oot, oot, oot,
If ev'ry little beetle stamped his foot
What an earthquake that would be.
>Stamp together with the whole wide world, [x3]
>What a great, great 'Quake!

I-if ev'ry little minnow flipped his tail, tail, tail
At the same same time, like a whale, whale, whale,
If ev'ry little minnow flipped his tail,
What a great wave that would be.
>Flip together with the whole wide world, [x3]
>What a great, great Wave!

I-if ev'ry human voice would sing a song, song, song
At the same same time, sing along, -long, -long
If ev'ry human voice would sing a song,
What a great choir that would be.
>Sing together with the whole wide world, [x3]
>What a great, great Choir

I-i-if ev'ry human heart would pray for peace, peace, peace
At the same, same time, never cease, cease, cease,
If ev'ry human heart would pray for peace
What a great peace that would be
>Sing Shalom an Halleluiah,
>I'm sure – ya a-gree,
>Hum-du-lillah, Hallelujah,
>What a great, great, peace

repeat last four lines.

CUDDLE
Nancy Nicolson

Cuddle

CHORUS
> *Cuddle, cuddle, cuddle against the war,*
> *Use your arms for cuddlin, that's what arms are for,*
> *Escalation could be bliss,*
> *Start off with a cuddle, end up with a kiss.*

Cuddle a Russian, peasant or tzar,
And he may show you his... samovar,
They say the Russians answer 'Niet',
I've never had that answer yet !

> *Cuddle, cuddle, ...*

Cuddle a Frenchman from Gay Paree,
Go and sit upon his knee,
Run your fingers through his hair,
And leave ze rest to Laissez-faire !

> *Cuddle, cuddle, ...*

I wrote 'Cuddle' in the mid-1980s. Some folk say that only Nuclear Arms will keep us safe, Others that only Conventional Arms will keep us safe. The ONLY arms that will keep us safe are fixed to our shoulders, and we got them for cuddling with. A friend reported some years ago that Cuddle was now "in the tradition" as he heard a new version at Sidmouth Folk Festival. It went: "Piddle, piddle, piddle against the wall ..." And Newcastle's lovely singer Di Henderson has been known to sing .'... Escalation could be luck, start off with a cuddle, end up ...!' Where is that girl going?

I seldom sing all the verses, rather select according to the company. Paddy Bort, of Edinburgh Folk Club, gave me the 'German' verse in 2013.

'Cuddle' and ' Do Nothing' were featured in Penny Stone's 2008 book *Now More than Ever, Here More Than Anywhere' 50 Years of Scottish Songs For Nuclear Disarmament*. Wee note to singers: Cuddle is an instruction, rather than a description. I have heard someone sing 'You cuddle a Russian'... etc. She sang it beautifully, but was missing the point. In my own view it's not such a strong message. However, if you are the singer, you are in charge, and I feel pleased when anyone chooses to sing one of my songs. Recorded on *Rhyme and Reason*, 1990.

Cuddle an Injun, do it with verve,
Break down that Brave's reserve,
Get into a big pow-wow,
I'm sure that he will show you 'How !'

Cuddle, cuddle, ...

Cuddle Australian, a wizard from Oz,
Lie on the beach with Santa Claus,
Rub his back with amber oils,
And wait until his Billy boils!

Cuddle, cuddle, ...

Cuddle a German, don't mention the War,
Go for a drive in his German car,
When on the Autobahn you click,
They call it "Vorsprung Durch Technik"!

Cuddle, cuddle,

Cuddle a Scotsman, he's Clydeside built,
Ask what's worn beneath the kilt
There's nothing worn North of the border,
Ma dear, it's all in working order!

Cuddle, cuddle, ..

LAST CAROL

Nancy Nicolson

INTRO.

Lo lo lo lo lo lo lo

REFRAIN

Mush-room cloud and hea-vy wat-er, My last son and your last daugh-ter;

White and sere the blast-ed ground, Hush-a, hush-a, all fall

VERSES

Merri-ly, mer-ri-ly down — nucle-ar pow — er, Merri-ly, mer-ri-ly

ki-lo-watt hour — Merry lit-tle factory for nuc-le-ar fu — el,

It will cook your merry goose and not your merry gru-el!

Last Carol

Mushroom cloud and heavy water,
My last son and your last daughter,
White and sere the blasted ground,
Husha, husha, all fall down.

    Merrily, merrily, nuclear power,
    Merrily, merrily, kilowatt hour,
    Merry little factory for nuclear fuel,
    It will cook your merry goose and not your merry gruel.

Merrily, merrily, scattering plutonium,
Always on my patch, never on your own one,
Set in merry glass and merry sunk in merry granite,
Can you merry, say it's merry safe? You merry cannot.

    Merrily, merrily, critical condition,
    Merrily, merrily, nuclear fission,
    Merry, merry, merry, merry, four-minute warning,
    Never, merry, not-a-merry-nother merry morning.

Written some time in the 1980s. When I sing this I sing 'Merry', but think 'Bloody'. Recorded on *Rhyme and Reason*, 1990.

POEMS AND A STORY

Garden Opens One Eye

Garden opens one eye one eye, one eye,
Garden opens one eye, Says, "I give you snowdrops".
Snowdrops, Snowdrops, peeping through the green,
What a long, long, winter it has been.
But Garden he grumbles, "Oh, Winter is deep."
And he pulls the covers over him and goes back to sleep

Garden opens two eyes, two eyes, two eyes,
Garden opens two eyes, says, "I give you crocuses."
Crocuses, Crocuses, in purple and in gold
Wave so bravely in the morning cold.
But Garden he grumbles, "Oh, Winter is deep."
And he pulls the covers over him and goes back to sleep.

Garden shakes his shoulders shoulders, shoulders,
Garden shakes his shoulders, says, "I give you daffodils."
Daffodils, Daffodils, dancing on the hill,
Laughing, laughing, never feel the chill.
But Garden he grumbles, "Oh, Winter is deep."
And he pulls the covers over him AND WE TICKLE HIS FEET

Garden jumps up giggling, giggling, giggling,
Garden jumps up giggling, blinks and rubs the sleep away...
Says ... I ... give ... you:
Tulips, primroses, corms and roots and seeds,
Dandelions, daisies, never call them weeds.
Herbs and grasses, speedwell in the lawn
Every trace of winter it is gone

And garden he chuckles, "Ah, Springtime is sweet,
Sunshine and raindrops to dance my old Feet."

Repeat last 2 lines

Written for Radio Scotland Schools Programme *Hopscotch*, producer Gerda Stevenson, in early 1990s.

Inverness Aunties

Auntie Jean and Auntie Maggie live in Inverness
They are each others' sisters, but you would never guess
For Auntie Jean is soft and smiley, quiet, kind and cuddly
And Auntie Mags is wild and loud, flashy, mad and muddly

Auntie Jean is tinkly and twinkly
When she smiles her rosy cheeks go crinkly
She stirs her tea with a silver spoon
And takes a nap in the afternoon

Auntie Mags is bangly and spangly
Likes her earrings dingly and dangly
With high-heeled shoes upon her feet
She whistles loudly in the street

Auntie Jean and Auntie Maggie live in Inverness
They are each others' sisters, but you would never guess
Auntie Jean and Auntie Maggie live in Inverness
They are each others' sisters, but you would never guess

A wee celebration of difference. Rhyme for *Hopscotch*, BBC Schools Programme, early 1990s.

Faa's Caat's Aat?

Faa's caat's aat wi e Muckle smurk? Tell me, fit's her neyme?
At peedie cat is a clever piece o work. Aat's e cat at got e creyme.

There's a cat at e palace wi a cheeky look, Geed an spat at e Queen
Cheysed e corgis, scratched e Duke. Aat's e Cat at Looked at a Keeng

Faa's cat's aat wi her whuskers burned? Too near e fire she sat,
Intil e very lowes she turned. Aat's E Cat aat Sat on e Mat

Faa's cat's aat all weet an dreepin, Climmin oot e well
Wisna cownin, wisna peepin. Lached an shook herself

Faa's cat's aat aat's yowlin sore up on e hey shed roof?
Went sailin oot e steyble door off a cloor fey a Clydesdale's hoof.

Climmed e hoose, fell off e lum. Aal she got, a bruise on e bum
Broke a leyg, hut by a bus. 'Wheesht', she says, 'Don't make a fuss'.

Chumped in e back o a dumper laary, Cowped wi a lod o stons in e quaary
Flattened by a beeg rod-roller, Joost geed wan indeegnant holler

Faa's cat's aat wi her tail half-chowed? Fit wis aat altercation?
Stupeed... Thocht she wis allowed Til chump on a Alsatian.

She met a monster in e dark, She got a aaful gluff
She didna dort, she didna nark, Said 'Monster! Aats anuff!'

Her eyes bloodshot, her body bruised, Looks lek she's cut wi knifes.
Oh, fowkies, hev ye no jaloused? Id's e Cat at Hes Nine Lives!

I was visiting village schools in Kaitness in May 2016, playing with some of the characteristic sounds in Kaitness language. I particularly like the broad 'aa' sound we have. In English the word 'ball' is pronounced as if it were spelled 'bawl'. In Caithness it is said as if spelled 'baal', to sound like 'shall'. Say this in English: Don't stand on that wall and play with a ball or you will fall! Now try it in Kaitness: Dinna staan on aat waal an play wi a baal or ye'll faal!

So fits e story, fits e tale? So brave an braa a cat.
A'm preegin w'ye, gie's yer craic. Hev ye no tweeged?

AAT'S MA CAT!!

Line Drawing by Denness Morton 'The Road to the Croft'

Hauf-Hinget Maggie

(The Story of Maggie Dickson)

Hauf-Hinget Maggie dee'ed an rose again
Hauf-Hinget Maggie didnae like the pain
'Let me up, let me oot, lowse the coffin door
Ahm no deid, an ma neck's sore!'

Maggie wis a fishwife, listen tae her caa
"Fine fat Haddies, fresh fae Fisherraw
Ma man's missin, God knows where
I miss kissin, Laddies, are ye there?"

Aff she's geen tae Kelsay, kissin did its stuff
She wisnae sic a bad lass, but just enough
Tae linger in the gloaming wi a sweet and tender boy
Tae hae a wee bit lovin, tae hae a wee bit joy.

Juist enough for a little seed tae set
Just   enough ... a babby for tae get,
An her a mairriet wumman, a sore an mortal sin!
She's flirtin wi the gallows, wi the gibbet's din.

She bore the little babby, but oh dear me
Wan way or anither, the babby, he did dee,
She left his wee bit body on the banks o the river
Sealed ... her ... fate for ever.

'Ther's gaun tae be a hingin!' see the scaffold nou
Stau-nin sterk, Gressmerket's fu
The faimily to wail, the crowd to see the fun
An medics seeking bodies when the deed is done.

Every word is true. Google and see the amazing story (1724). A pub in the Grassmarket is named
after Maggie Dickson – so her name and story will be remembered for some time yet.

They say the rope was weak, they say the knot was slack
Maggie freed her hans fae the cord ahint her back.
Tuggin at the loose noose, she implored
'Ah didnae dae it ... an ma neck's sore!'

The crowd they stoned the hangman for failin in his task.
Tae hing a wee bit lassie, is that too much tae ask?
Again he hung her, an he strung her, an he kicked awa the board
The lassie dropped, her breath it stopped, the haill crowd roared.

The hangman pu'ed her heels doon, made shair at she wis deid,
Her mither screamed, her brither roared, her faither held his heid.
The medics tried tae snatch her tae tak tae Surgeon's Ha.
Her brither James he punched their faces up against the wa.

They nailed her in a coffin and set her on a cairt,
And took the road tae Inveresk wi mony heavy hert.
At Peffermill they hud a rest fae cairtin their sad load,
To hae a jug o ale, an left the coffin by the road.

Twae jiners at wis passin saw the coffin there
An took a look tae check the joints, thae dovetails, are they square?
What's that? Was that a thumpin? They surely heard a knock
They ran to tell the faimily, at nearly Dee'ed o shock.

Twae claw hammers caaed aff the coffin heid
Up shot Maggie, onythin but deid.
'Man whit kept ye?,' she did roar,
'Ah'm no deid ... an ma neck's sore!'

Some said Maggie let her baby dee
She said she didnae, that's good enough for me.
Guid Loard abeen, he kent the score.
Maggie didnae dae it, He oped the coffin door

Nou she's walkin an she's talkin, and tossin her fine heid.

Scots Law says she was hinget, therefore she is deid.
Her merriage is annulled, and aa her sins forgiven.
Maggie's here on Scotland's soil, Sivinth Heaven.

Her man he heard the story, his heid was in a whiril
Maggie, that's ma lassie, what a giril!
Maggie ... watched him ... comin up the lane,
The fine lad, the canny lad, she mairried him again

An they had bonnie bairnies, a long contented life,
This time the man took-better-care-o-his-good-wife.
She lived on in Edinburry full forty years an more...
Saying, 'Ahm no deid ... and ma neck's sore!'

The Lesson

A Caithness dialogue between Davey, 9, and his Mam

M: Fit's up, Davey?
D: Nothin

M: I'ds no nothin
D: Weel, nearly nothin – A got a row

M: Fa fey?
D: Fey e teycher

M: Fit for?
D: For sayin somethin

M:An fit did ye say?
D: Owld wifie.

M:Ye caalled him a owld wifie?
D: No-oh (*say 'o' as in gone*)

M:Fit then?
D: A sayed 'owld wifie' when A wis speakin til him

M:Bit ye ken ye shouldna speak til e teycher lek at!
D: A ken

M:So fit did ye do'd fir?
D: Weel A thocht he wanted me til speak lek at

M:Oh Davey!
D: A ken, bit we wiz doin creative writin – no doin id really – joost gettin ready for id – e speakin bittie. Id started off wi him readin hiz a story – id wis good. Id wis caaled 'The Old Woman's Dilemma' – and she hed three sons an a croft an she wis aaful poor an richt honest. Wan day e owldest son wis oot workin an he horted himsel and he wis lek til dee – bit they hed no money til get a doctor – an ere she wis, – joost desperate!

Written 1990. This is essentially the same story as the song 'Listen to the Teacher', I just thought I'd like to 'take it home' to get Mam's side on it. Recorded on *Rhyme and Reason*,1990.

E yoowngest chiel sayed they hed til get some money, an he kent far til get id – there wis a sovereign in a box in e Baron's castle. Bit e mither sayed 'No-oh, at wid be steylin.' An e middle chiel sayed fit else could they do? An e mither sayed she didna ken, bit they mustna steyl.

An e yowngest chiel sayed, 'Weel, Fit wid be worst – steylin e money or letting their brither dee?

Id wis aal in iss book he hed – e usual thing, aal posh – 'Once upon a time in land far away, lived an old woman who had three sons, very dear to her' tra-la-la.

An how e row happened wis iss – efter he reads e whole lot, he bangs e book shut and says, 'Right you lot – the whole story, and what you think the old woman does – IN YOUR OWN WORDS'

An he looks strecht at me – so A says, 'Weel, there wis iss owld wifie.'.

An he goes off e heyd – roarin lek a bull. 'Less of your cheek – I'll have no lipp from you. Where do you think you are – the top of Newton Hill?

We're civilized down here and we speak like civilised people. We'll have proper English in this classroom and none of your slipshod rubbish!'

He meyd a richt fool o me fornent e whole class. Now they're aal laughin at me.

M: (Smilin) An aat's fit's botherin ye?
D: Aye – no e row

M: (still smilin) Poor Davey, at's a sheyme
D: Id's aal richt … Id wis ma ain faalt.

He did say 'In your own words', bit A should've min't he wis e teycher. A shud've kent he didna mean id.

Id wis ma ain faalt.

END

GLOSSARY

Pronounciation: 'u' is usually said as in up, not as in put.
'a' is usually said as in can, not as in call.

This list is based on 'A Hundred Words in Kaitness Language' that I selected as a Scots Language Ambassador in Schools.
*words starred are not of the hundred, but appear in the Book.

*aat: that

abeen: above

ablow: below

aikle: molar tooth

ailiss: fierce fire

airt: direction

*an: and

antle: to harp on, to nag

*at: that

aumrie: cupboard

*aye: yes

*barrie; braw, good (Edinburgh language)

*beeg: big

ben: through *(to the other room)*

bere: a primitive form of barley (*say' bare'*)

besom: sweeping brush

bink: bench, work-top

birl: whirl, revolve

birss: hackles, temper

bisom: unpleasant woman

blackjock: blackbird

blin-drift: blinding dry powdery snow

blockie: a young cod

bool: a big stone

boorach: shambles

bowg: wyme, stomach

box: butt with head, of an animal

*boyagie: wee boy

*breeg: bridge

browg: awl, tool to make holes in leather *(brogue)*

by-name: nickname

*canna: can't

chantie po: chamber pot (Fr. singing pot)

*chiel: man

*choost: just

*chum: to accompany

clapshot: mix of cooked tatties an neeps *(stress second syllable)*

clype: scratch

cown: cry, weep

*creytur: creature

*dee: die

dicht: quick wipe

* downg: dung

drocht: good drying wind

drookid: of a person, soaked

*dunt: blow

*eygs: eggs

*fey: from

 *fit?: what?

flech: flea

*flit: move house (Kaitness and Scots language)

foosum: filthy

fornent: (situated) in front of

*fowk: folk

*fun: found

gaapus: loud-mouthed person

gandy-goes: nonsense, mischief

gant: stutter

*gie, gied: give, gave

gluff: a sudden fright

Good-: in-law, eg Good-mither, Good-brither

gowk: fool, idiot

gowpen: two hands cupped

grice: piglet

grushen: fringe (of hair)

gushel: messy, with liquid

gutters: mud

gyo: goe; steep narrow inlet of the sea, eg Whaligoe

hallan: partition between animals' stalls

heels-abeen: head-over-heels

***heidie:** headmaster (Kaitness and Scots language)

***hid:** it

***hill: moorland** (although it's as flat as a pancake)

hirple: hobble

***hiz:** us

***hort:** hurt

***jalouse:** deduce

***Kaitness:** Caithness

keich: turd

***ken:** know

kirn: churn

kist: chest, box

***lassagie:** wee girl

***lek:** like

***lok:** lot, large amount

***looger:** a slap on the ear

***ma:** my

marakless: gormless, careless (of a person)

***mind/mind on:** remember

***mischievious:** mischievous (say it with four syllables – make a meal of it!)

moniment: rascal

neep: turnip

nether: adder, snake

 ***neyme:** name

nippid: of clothing, on the tight side

nyirl: complain in whining voice

*o: of

oo: loose sheep's wool

oxter: underarm

park: field

partan: crab

pech: to pant

peedie: little

peep: to cry, weep

peepag: whistle made of grass or corn stalk

*perchink: fussily prim

pirn: reel (of thread)

purr: thorn

quoy: a heifer

raivel: ravel, muddle

rillins: in ragged strips

rive: to pull roughly, to tear

roup: farm sale

*sayed: said (the vowel is long, as in prayed)

scarf or **skarf**: cormorant

scon: flatten

scorrie-scoot: gull droppings

scroo: stack of hay or straw

sharn: cows' dung

shither: folk, the people of an area

shochad: peewit, lapwing

simmon: rope made of hay or straw

skibbie-lickie: tig, (bairns' game)

skifter: a light covering of snow

skint: a wee drop of liquid

skirl: scream, screech

skook: sneak with head and shoulders down

slock: put out, extinguish

sneck: latch

sneeter: snigger

soorag: sorrel

*spek: speak, speaking, language

sprowg: sparrow

spurtle: stick for stirring porridge

swack: lithe

sweer: loath, unwilling

swick: cheat swindle

*tatties: potatoes (Kaitness and Scots language)

teem: to pour

teet: to peep, look quickly

*til: to

toch-toch: a call to cattle to come [**shook-shook** – horse; **pet-pet** –
           sheep; **tick-tick** – hens; **grice-grice** - pig]

trig: neat, trim

twite: whittle (of wood)

*wan: one

*wean: child (Glasgow, wee ane)

*weer: wire

*wi: with

*wur: our

wurshid: worsted, wool, yarn. (*Say 'u' as in up.*)

*yowes: ewes

*yowng: young

SONG TITLES and *First Lines*

CONTRIBUTORS

Eberhard 'Paddy' Bort works at the University of Edinburgh's Academy of Government. He is Chair of Edinburgh Folk Club and runs the Wee Folk Club at The Royal Oak. He has edited four volumes anent Hamish Henderson with Grace Note Publications.

Brian Craib was born in 1943 in Kirriemuir, Angus, the eldest son of a jute-mill weaver (mother) & farm labourer (father). After leaving school aged 17, he worked briefly as a shoe salesman in Dundee, then for four years as a trainee management accountant for the Rank Organisation. But around July, 1965, he became very bored with it and decided to try to become a professional musician. (He had begun at the age of 15 to teach himself the double bass and was now playing in amateur orchestras and also in a jazz quintet called the Full-Tone 5, which later became the Average White Band.) His intention was to become a student at the Royal Academy in Glasgow, but someone persuaded him to audition for a new orchestra which the BBC were starting in Bristol. To his utter amazement, he was given the third out of four jobs (there were 34 applicants) so he spent 1966 in Bristol. A year later, he was taken on by the SNO, and became Assistant Principal a year later. He resigned in 1970 (the politics bored him!) and was offered a teaching job in Aberdeen. Subsequently, he taught for two years in Glasgow, and seven years in his home county and, from 1980 until his retiral in 2008, in Fife.

George Gunn is best known as a poet and playwright from Caithness. He has written for BBC Scotland and Radio 4 and has had numerous articles, poems and essays published in magazines, journals and newspapers. He was a founding director of the Grey Coast Theatre Company from 1992 to 2010 and tutors in Drama at North Highland College. His latest publication is a lyrical, heartfelt portrait of the far north of Scotland – a poet's journey through Caithness: *The Province of the Cat* (Islands Book Trust, 2015).

Ewan McVicar, like Nancy Nicolson born 75 years ago in the North, lives part of the time in a Lithca research library, and partly in a flat over a Cromba bookshop. He has written many songs for adults and with children, made books and recordings and websites, and told tales around Alba and in foreign lands.

Gerda Stevenson is an award-winning actor/writer/director/singer/songwriter. Her work has been widely staged, broadcast and published throughout Britain and abroad; recipient of writers' bursaries from the Scottish Arts Council and Creative Scotland. Her play *FEDERER VERSUS MURRAY* (pub. *Salmagundi* (USA), toured to New York in 2012; her poetry collection *If This Were Real* was published by Smokestack Books, 2013. Nominated as Scots Singer of the Year, for her album of her own songs, *NIGHT TOUCHES DAY,* 2014. Has written extensively for BBC radio, including a drama about asylum seekers and refugees, to be broadcast 2017; currently completing her second poetry collection. www.gerdastevenson.co.uk

RHYME AND REASON

Getting Some of Nancy's Songs Down on Tape

Ewan McVicar

In 1989 I started my record label, Gallus, with an LP of old and new songs of Glasgow. The second Gallus issue was one I was bound and determined to create. I had met Nancy Nicolson on various politically committed platforms, and been mightly impressed by the high quality of her songmaking and singing, and the warmth of her engagement with audiences. It felt important to make her songs available to be learned and performed by others, and I was sure there were more of her songs to be shared than the political ones I knew about.

I think she was uncertain of what I could do, but she was willing to have a go. I hired Tower Studios in Glasgow, a small gloom-shrouded recording studio up a grubby back lane, tucked in under the tower of the high Free Church building on top of Park Terrace. At the time I was pretty much their only paying client; the proprietor, Craig Tannock, was working to promote and manage emerging rock bands. When faced with recording Nancy singing unaccompanied Craig decided, why I did not comprehend, to use two microphones, one aimed at her mouth and the other at her throat. We recorded several songs, but when listening back extra-carefully we learned that Nancy, and for ought I ken, other singers, have a curious click in their throats when singing. The first set of recordings had to be junked. We started again, more successfully. Nancy decided what songs were to be more than solo affairs, and after a couple of days she brought in Derek Moffat of the McCalmans to play guitar and sing backing vocals. She had often performed with him in Edinburgh settings, she told me, and Derek stormed through his songs with her in fine style, never a retake needed. I managed to plunk a nylon strung guitar backing for a couple of the other songs, Nancy did a little double-tracking on 'Last Carol', and she played a few tunes on her melodeon, but there were two pieces that called for more atmospheric treatment.

I had worked before on various projects with Alan Tall, former member of Wildcat Theatre in Glasgow and a remarkable musician and composer. I brought him in to create strong and affecting arrangements on keyboard and flute, particularly for 'The Mistress'. As Nancy and I sat huddled in Tower Studios' control room listening to the gale-swept keyboard accompaniment he was creating for Nancy's song track, she gripped my hand vicelike. The quality of that arrangement was shown later when Ed Miller, Texas-based Scots exile singer, used almost the same sounds when he chose to record Nancy's song.

Many another songmaker would have packed only their own work into their first recording, but, generous as always, not all the songs chosen by Nancy were her own composition. 'Pigs Can See The Wind' was written by Dave Goulder, 'Mither Mither' by Sheila Douglas, and 'Dark Island' was composed by Iain MacLachlan.

When the recordings were ready for release, I had learned to my cost that the sales of LPs had collapsed, so the album was released on cassette only. In the last few years Nancy and I have also made it available on CD. The cassette notes began with a quotation from one of our best music journalists. "Nancy writes songs that are cunningly temperate," said Alastair Clark of *The Scotsman*. I added, "Sly humour, moving lyricism, catchy tunes, singable choruses. Songs that pack a well-aimed punch. Eleven original songs and a story, plus two from other writers, and a few tunes on melodeon. Nancy says if you like the songs, sing them."

Within the cassette insert, beside an alarmingly grainy photo of Nancy, we wrote, "Nancy Nicolson is an Edinburgh-based singer and songwriter originally from Caithness whose work is widely known on the folk scene, but who, until now, has never had an album to call her own." Then we added a longer piece from Alastair Clark.

"Through her own singing and the readiness of other singers and bands to pick up her material – just recently Leon Rosselson phoned her from London to make sure that he was using the right tune to one of her pieces – some of her compositions have travelled far and wide.

"Like many of her political songs, which tend to be coded in overtly charming allegorical form, 'Don't Call Maggie A Cat' has almost a nursery-rhyme air about it – a quality that emerges, too, in 'The Eagle And The Bear', which is, beneath the blithe imagery, a heavy number about the international power struggle. 'Hard Boiled Eggs', which tackles the food-poisoning controversy, and, above all, 'Last Carol', a song of nuclear apocalypse, carry a full quota of polemical power.

"And she's an extremely versatile writer too, able to produce a touching love song like 'Keepingsakes' and a delightful defence of hame-spun dialect in 'Listen Tae The Teacher', as well as a darkly poetic song of the sea, 'The Mistress'.

"All this is delivered in a youthful, bright, clear voice that never shows a hint of strain or indecision. It amounts to a great collection by one of the outstanding folk talents of our day." [Alastair Clark in *The Scotsman*, 20 January 1990].

Nancy expressed her own thanks, ending in typically sly fashion: "My thanks to my Dad, Bill, uncles Eann Nicolson and Sandy Stewart for music long ago, to the Edinburgh Folk Club who started me rhyming, and to friends at the Royal Oak, Edinburgh, for all kinds of support. To Ewan and all involved in this recording – bless ye, I aye kent ye were daft."

The cassette, titled *Rhyme And Reason* and featuring a striking cover image of a quill pen dripping ink made by Nancy's husband Denness, sold well, and helped to spread performance of her songs. Every now and then I would be in her audience, or she in mine, or both of us on stage. I would get to hear of her doings, and once I visited her primary school class to sing and make up verses, where I saw first hand her remarkable empathy with and love for her charges.

It is an ongoing frustration for me that she has not gone on to record and get released her newer (newer than 1990!) songs, other than a couple made with school pupils for New Makars Trust project in Fife.

The one other song of hers sung by her that I know made it on to vinyl was one she would not put on the *Rhyme and Reason* album because its criticism of police actions during the 1986 Miners' Strike had been a source of pain to her good friend Ian Green of Greentrax records, himself an ex-policeman. Although 'Maggie's Pit Ponies' had not made the selection committee's cut for the final competition performance of the annual national Songsearch songwriting competition organised by singer and activist Bob Pegg, he liked

Nancy's song so much he smuggled it on to the LP of finalist songs anyway.

As you would expect, Nancy's telling of how the song came to be made is a fine tale in itself, which she told me for my book, *The Eskimo Republic.*

Here come the cavalry, here come the troops
Here come Maggie's Pit Ponies
Watch for the batons and watch for the boots
And watch your back, Miner Johnnie

Nancy's bus to work passed the road-end where there were pickets for Bilston Glen colliery.

"It was just heartrending seeing these guys standing there. Then, at a teachers' meeting in Edinburgh we were watching a piece of newsreel, of horses running into and through a picket line. My friend said, 'Those bloody horses'. I said, 'The horses are just doing what they were trained to do.' And I looked at the boys on their backs, doing what they were trained to do. I told my husband Denness, and he said, 'Aye, some bloody pit ponies'. The song just grew itself.

"I sang it at a concert, an this fine lookin man in a suit came marchin towards me, I thought 'I've done it, this is the day I'm gonnae get bopped in the face'. He says, 'That song,'– I says 'What song?' 'The miners' song, where'd ye get it?' I put my chin up ready to be hit and said, 'I wrote it.' He took me by the lapels to be even closer, and he says, 'On the button, hen! On the button!' He was Jackie Aitchison, one of the miners' leaders."

I have done a lot of stuff in my time, but getting just some of Nancy's songs down on tape and out there for others is among my top five achievements.

FURTHER BOOK RESOURCES
RHYME AND REASON PLUS

Nancy Nicolson's 1990 tape, recorded by Ewan McVicar and originally issued on his Gallus label, with new recordings (marked with an asterix) made by David O'Leary live at Edinburgh Folk Club in September and October 2016.

01.	E Man At Muffed Id	3' 25"
02.	The Mistress	4' 04"
03.	Don't Call Maggie a Cat	1' 50"
04.	Last Carol	2' 50"
05.	Who Pays the Piper?	3' 19"
06.	Hard-Boiled Eggs	2' 28"
07.	Listen tae the Teacher	3' 02"
08.	The Lesson	3' 10"
09.	The Heilan Horse	3' 37"
10.	The Keepingsakes	3' 31"
11.	The Eagle and the Bear	3' 08"
12.	Cuddle	4' 40"
13.	Maggie's Pit Ponies*	3' 17"
14.	The Brickie's Ballad*	2' 28"
15.	Don't Waste Ma Time*	3' 12"
16.	The Moon in the Morning*	3' 08"
17.	They Sent a Wumman*	3' 27"
18.	Faa's Caat's Aat?*	2' 21"

HOW TO OBTAIN FURTHER BOOK RESOURCES: The resource tracks listed in this page can be obtained as downloads by writing to Grace Note Publications at ***books@gracenotereading.co.uk*** or through the publisher website: <***www.gracenotepublications.co.uk***>.

On the original tracks you will hear the guitar accompaniment of Ewan McVicar, the atmospheric keyboard accompaniment of Allan Tall and the vocal and guitar accompaniment of the irreplaceable Derek Moffat.

'I hear Derek with his wonderful harmonies and guitar, and he is alive again, beside me, smiling, encouraging. Bless you, Derek. For me he still lives in this work. Art and Music are eternal in their life-affirming elements.'

Nancy Nicolson

Printed in Great Britain
by Amazon